A FEW WORDS IN THE DARK

St. Valentines Day
2018, 14 February

Dearest Marie,

Love the Light

Forever

∞

and you can get
through anything . . .
and out the other side!

Dad

Kagawa Toyohiko

A FEW WORDS IN THE DARK
Selected Meditations

Translated and Annotated by

Thomas John Hastings

BRIDGES TO PEACE PUBLICATIONS
PRINCETON, N.J.

This publication was made possible through the support of a grant from the John Templeton Foundation. The views expressed in this publication are those of the author and do not necessarily reflect the views of the John Templeton Foundation.

cover photo by Tim Boyle

ISBN 978-1-517-01049-2

Design and typesetting: Nanzan Institute for Religion and Culture, Nagoya, Japan

Contents

Remembering Kagawa Toyohiko (1888–1960)
A Brief Biography

Any American who attended a mainline Protestant church between 1925 and 1960 almost certainly would have heard of Toyohiko Kagawa (or Kagawa Toyohiko in the Japanese rendering that places family name first). A quick search of the limited online archive of *The Christian Century* from 1940 until his death in 1960 yields 35 articles that mention the once world-renowned Japanese evangelist, social reformer, writer, and Nobel Prize nominee (Literature twice, Peace Prize four times).

Chronicling his anguished childhood, teenage baptism, and dramatic decision to follow Christ by moving into Kobe's worst slum in 1909, his 1920 semi-autobiographical *Shisen wo koete*[1] seized the imagination of an entire generation of Japanese readers, becoming the best selling novel of the Taishō Era (1912–1926). With the 1924 publication of the English translation, this legendary convert of American Southern Presbyterian missionaries and graduate of the Princeton Theological Seminary class of 1916 was destined to become a poster child for foreign missionary efforts in Japan. But news of the so-called "saint of the Kobe slum" spread quickly beyond the religious world. For example, beginning with Gardner Harding's July 1923 laudatory piece, "Powerful Spiritual Leaders Wake Japan from Materialism," Kagawa is mentioned in more than ninety subsequent New York Times articles up until his death in 1960.[2]

---

1. Literally *Across the Death Line*, or *Before the Dawn* in the English translation. *Before the Dawn*. Translated by I. Fukumoto and T. Satchell. New York: Doran, 1924.
2. New York Times Online Archive: http://query.nytimes.com/search/.

9

Along with a small circle of young associates, Kagawa and his life-long co-worker and spouse Haru began their work in anonymity among Kobe's poorest inhabitants, but after the success of the novel, instead of settling into a comfortable lifestyle, they opted to invest all of the substantial royalties into an ambitious evangelical and social reform movement that jump-started several evangelistic, social, educational, publishing, and medical projects and institutions on behalf of the poor, children, laborers, consumers, women, and farmers. According to Ōta Yūzō, by 1940 the Kagawas were responsible for "4 settlement houses, 6 cooperatives, 6 slum kitchens, 3 hospitals, 17 kindergartens, 3 tuberculosis sanitaria, 3 gospel schools, 1 domestic science school, 2 magazines, a farm, and 19 churches."[3] This grassroots movement boldly tackled pressing social problems such as unemployment, hunger, sickness, lack of education for urban poor and farmers, etc. These efforts were often not understood and sometimes even ridiculed by leaders of the established churches where Kagawa maintained his credentials as an ordained Presbyterian minister. As Kagawa biographer Sumiya Mikio points out, this "religious movement was a progressive reform movement against the churches who restricted faith to the spiritual world and enshrined the gospel in the church alone."[4]

Though widely revered by the general public and often compared to his contemporaries Gandhi and Schweitzer, Kagawa was and remains an anomaly in the history of Japanese Protestantism, which after almost 160 years of massive foreign and indigenous efforts is still predominantly an individualistic, urban, middle-class phenomenon. Inspired by the abolitionism and prison reform movement of the Methodists and the gradualist, cooperative economic ideals of the Rochdale Weavers and British Guild Socialists, Kagawa was

---

3. Ōta Yūzō, "Kagawa Toyohiko: A Pacifist?" in *Pacifism in Japan: The Christian and Socialist Tradition* (Vancouver: University of British Columbia Press, 1978), 172.

4. Sumiya Mikio, *Kagawa Toyohiko* [in Japanese] (Tokyo: Iwanami), 2011, 170.

considered an outlier for equally emphasizing evangelical preaching and practical social reform. Especially since the student rebellion of the late 1960's and early 1970's, the mainline Protestant churches in Japan are still sharply divided into hardened factions ("social gospel" *shakaiha* and "church gospel" *kyōkaiha*), evidence that they rejected Kagawa's more holistic way. But while his work as a social reformer is unrivaled in the history of twentieth-century Japan, it is often forgotten that Kagawa was from first to last a determined, itinerant evangelist making his gospel appeal to a nation bent on achieving— no matter the cost—rapid industrialization and militarization in order to compete with Western imperial and colonial powers.

Though an exceptionally bright student and voracious reader, he abandoned an early academic interest in historical critical approaches to the Bible to preach and live out his vision for this vital unity between spiritual and social reform. More than three hundred books and translations were published in his name during his lifetime, and though he had a gift for writing, he also suffered from trachoma, a chronic eye disease he contracted in the slum. Consequently, many of his writings are actually transcriptions of his speeches, sermons, and lectures by a team of devoted co-workers. On aggregate, the writings reveal Kagawa as a kind of "professorial evangelist" who took on the entire nation as his classroom or congregation. He was especially well read in the natural sciences, philosophy of religion, and psychology, but after his seminary studies did not give much time to systematic or dogmatic theology, since he had no patience for abstract debates that failed to connect to the pressing social, political, economic, psychological, moral, and spiritual issues of his hearers and readers.

It must be said that he filtered everything through his daily spiritual practice of Scripture reading, prayer, and silent meditation. This regular spiritual discipline was the wellspring of his unbounded energy and confidence, which enabled him to take a broad, mystical view of things that enboldend him to see merit in positions others

considered contradictory. He could creatively fuse aspects of traditional Reformed theology with certain Neo-Confucian and Buddhist
teachings, interrogate assumptions in continental philosophy using
the latest findings in quantum mechanics, or criticize philosophical influences on evolutionary theory from a personalist perspective.
Rather than simply translating the latest intellectual trends from the
West into Japanese, Kagawa proclaimed a gospel for the Japanese
people centered on Christ's "redemptive love" and practical ethic of
"collective responsibility," utilizing the familiar linguistic, aesthetic,
religious, philosophical, and ethical ways of knowing in which he
and his audiences had been nurtured. While many of his peers in
the Protestant intellectual world had fallen under the spell of German dialectical theology and existential philosophy, Kagawa chose a
more apologetic, correlational, or contextual approach, in the spirit
of Clement of Alexandria, Paul Tillich, or Martin Luther King, Jr.

This approach comes through clearly in the present volume,
which is a selection of meditations from Kagawa's 1926 *A Few Words
in the Dark*.[5] You will notice, for example, that he freely utilizes Buddhist terms in making his point. Rather than rejecting or ignoring
the linguistic and conceptual worlds evoked by Japan's spiritual heritage, two strategies pursued by many foreign missionaries and Japanese Christian theologians, he had a deep sense of respect for the
power of that rich and varied heritage and believed the gospel would
never take root in Japan without positively engaging it. Of course,
this was exactly the approach of the early Christian apologists who
highjacked certain core Hellenistic concepts, such as *paideia*, when
making their evangelical appeal.

Kagawa's personalist, holistic, and apologetic approach may
again be relevant in our own time of increasing religious plural-

---

5. Original title: Kagawa Toyohiko 賀川豊彦, *Anchū sekigo* 『暗中隻語』 (Tokyo:
Shunjusha, 1926, 3rd edition). Please note that the numbers following each selection in
the Table of Contents and the main text correspond to those in the original.

ism, when we are beginning to see a new willingness among some religious practitioners and theologians to learn from other traditions. One beautiful example of this more open spirit is Pentecostal theologian Amos Yong, who says in regard to his own tradition, "A Christian theology of nature can and must learn from the sciences and other wisdom traditions, including Buddhism."[6] As in Kagawa's time, there is little doubt that the methodologies and assumptions of modern science will continue to challenge ancient faith traditions in different ways. As a sophisticated theological and philosophical response to such challenges, Yong pursues what he calls a "Christianity-Buddhism-Science trialogue" on basic questions of "spirit" and "nature." Indeed, Kagawa and other Christian converts in the non-western world may be read as early exemplars of the kind of "trialogue" Yong and others advocate, for as someone steeped in Japan's Shinto, Buddhist, and Neo-Confucian ethos, he was also thoroughly up to date on the "Western" intellectual developments of his time. The key point, however, is that Kagawa was trying to sort out the specific terms of the "trialogue"—Christianity, Japan's spiritual heritage, and science—as a Christian evangelist and social reformer.

As you read these selections, you will be struck by Kagawa's audacious determination and belief that he could put Christ's "redemptive love" and "collective responsibility" into concrete practice in his own life and, by extension, in Japanese society. He took his religious identity and calling with a degree of urgency reminiscent of the early Christian missionaries who set out to evangelize the ancient world beyond Palestine. When asked what Jesus was like, Kagawa reportedly responded, "Follow me and find out," like the Apostle Paul who had admonished wayward Corinthians to "Be imitators of me, as I am of Christ." (I Co 11:1)

6. Amos Yong, *The Cosmic Breath: Spirit and Nature in the Christianity-Buddhism-Science Trialogue* (Brill, 2012), 29.

Kagawa was in no way wedded to theological traditions he judged as outmoded or overly speculative. For example, even though he had cut his theological teeth on the old-school Calvinism at Kobe Theological School (class of 1911) and Princeton Theological Seminary (class of 1916), he was committed to progress in religion and science and was therefore willing to reject or disregard contestable doctrines such as "total depravity" or "double predestination." Rather, seeking to press Darwin's powerful theory—with certain critical caveats—into service to the present and coming Kingdom of God, he held to a basically optimistic view of human beings and human potential, believing that Scripture, Neo-Confucian teaching, evolutionary biology, and common sense all supported a trajectory of spiritual evolution in creatures endowed with self-consciousness, conscience, and a degree of free will. Rather than wasting time and energy debating the ultimate fate of the elect and the depraved, he set to work with a brazen assurance that the natural graces of humanity only awaited the mediation of the Holy Spirit to achieve Christ's "full consciousness" of "redemptive love" and "collective responsibility."

As one might expect, his failure at times to achieve such a lofty spiritual ambition made him an easy target for certain well-deserved criticisms after he died. The most serious condemnation came in regard to his brief, but harsh discriminatory characterizations of the *Buraku* in his early *A Study of the Psychology of the Poor* (1915). The *Buraku* are a Japanese minority long victimized for their participation in occupations once considered ritually impure, and Kagawa's early comments reveal that he had swallowed the theory of racial origins proposed by Ernst Haeckel, Francis Galton, and others, a theory supported by many of the world's intellectuals of the time.[7]

---

7. One good examination of the elitist contempt for the masses is John Carey's expose of these views among British literary elites. While Carey does not touch on Japan in this context, Kagawa makes reference to many of the writers Carey mentions; i.e., H. G. Wells, G. B. Shaw, Ezra Pound, James Joyce, E. M Forster, Virginia Woolf, T. S.

In spite of this serious flaw in his early thinking, it also needs to be said that Kagawa remained a lifelong champion of the most vulnerable members of society. In fact, Japanese theologian Kuribayashi Teruo suggests one sociological cause of the rift between Kagawa and "established" church leaders and theologians was the "proto-liberationist" motif in the evangelical social reformer's views. Reflecting on Kagawa's theology on the 2009 centennial commemoration of the move into the Kobe slum, Kuribayashi says,

> If we think of the boast of Uemura Masahisa, the leader of the Japanese church in the Meiji and Taishō Eras, who said, "My churches don't need the likes of rickshaw drivers or factory workers," Kagawa proclaimed, "The poorest of the poor are the heart of the church. The most obscure must become the treasure of the church," it is no surprise that pastors did not welcome him. When Kagawa said, "Faith is not about intellectually swallowing the creeds," it is no surprise he was not viewed favorably by Japan's systematic theologians.[8]

Kagawa was ordained in the (Presbyterian) Church of Christ in Japan and had close ties with leaders of the other mainline denominations during his leadership of the Kingdom of God Movement, a program for mass evangelization and commitment to social reform that he launched in 1926 and pursued tirelessly until the early 1930's. But given the strategic and ideological differences with the "established" churches, as well as Kagawa's sometimes provocative and even arrogant tone, it is not surprising that the Japanese churches quickly forgot about him after his death in 1960. The legacy of this rupture in the Protestant movement is still borne out in Japan today where one often finds more Kagawa sympathizers within the consumer cooperative movement he helped to found than in the established

Eliot and others. John Carey, *The Intellectual and the Masses: Pride and Prejudice among the Literary Intelligentsia 1880–1939* (Chicago: Academy, 1992).

8. Kuribayashi, Teruo, "Rereading Kagawa's Theology in the Midst of a Recession," [in Japanese], Quarterly at 15 (2009) 55.

churches and seminaries. Given this background and the fact that only 20 of his books were translated into now out of print English editions, Kagawa also has been forgotten in the English-speaking world.

While he should be honored for his prophetic witness and lasting contributions as a social reformer, I hope these meditations will show that he should be remembered also for his lifelong search for a positive rapprochement between religion or spirituality and natural science, an important theme in his work that has not received adequate attention in or beyond Japan. Kagawa's voice deserves to be heard and situated in his own context as a creative Japanese evangelist, social reformer, and interdisciplinary thinker. He defines his basic stance on religion and science in one of the meditations included below, saying,

> I am a scientific mystic. The more scientific I am, the more I feel that I am penetrating deeply into God's world. Especially in the domain of biology do I feel as though I am talking face to face with God. Through life, I discover purpose even in a mechanical world. Science is the mystery of mysteries. It is the divine revelation of revelations.[9]

Kagawa retained the old Reformed theology of "general revelation" but took it a step further, believing that the scientific observation of nature reveals something of the divine nature when positioned against the larger background of the emergence of life and consciousness out of matter in the vast universe. He called Christ's cross and resurrection "the reality of the repair of the cosmos" and saw hints, instantiations, or analogies of divine agency in the subtlety or fine-tuning of restorative mechanisms operating in the natural world.

This "scientific mystic" sought to harmonize a robust and open-minded Christian faith with a deep and abiding interest in the latest

9. *A Few Words in the Dark*, (81).

findings in the natural sciences, and most especially developments in evolutionary biology and quantum physics. Given his sense of vocation, it is not surprising that his interest in science, like his work as a social reformer, was driven by a contextual, evangelical motive. Introduced in Japan in the late nineteenth century, evolutionary theory was sometimes thought to support a radical materialism and notion of purposelessness that Kagawa and other observers saw as hostile both to Christianity and to other Japanese religions. In response to this background, he writes,

> So closely do the Japanese feel themselves akin to nature and her ways that their thought of God takes on cosmic dimensions. Therefore, to bring home to the Japanese Christ's revelation of God as Father we must teach, as Ostwald does, that matter also has definite direction. We must show, as Driesch does, that there is harmony among organic bodies. We must stress the fact, as J. H. Fabre does, that God's purpose is built even into animal intuition. If we fail to make these things convincingly clear the Japanese will not believe in a God of love. Even the urbanized Japanese are never weaned from nature. A religion, therefore, which fails to interpret nature will not win their allegiance. No matter how much they are taught regarding human love, unless shown that there is love in nature they will not find faith possible.[10]

Soon after completing his studies in 1916 at Princeton Theological Seminary and Princeton University, where he enrolled in advanced courses in theology and evolution, psychology, mathematics, mammalian evolution, and genetics, he had pretty much settled on his conviction that modern science needed religion as much as religion needed science.

As we will see in the writings collected here, he freely employs a broad range of religious, philosophical, and scientific voices to assert

---

10. Toyohiko Kagawa, *Christ and Japan*, translated by William Axling (New York: Friendship, 1934), 40–41.

the importance of the enduring partnership between the religious contemplation and scientific observation of the cosmos. While more often taunting Japanese theologians for their neglect of science, here is an example of one of his stinging admonitions to Japanese scientists, written in 1946 on the heals of ww II.

> There is no religion in Japan's natural sciences, and cosmology is missing. As a result, scientists befriend only other like-minded scientists and attack those who disagree with them, becoming narrow-minded, settling for trivialities and making little progress.
>
> When Mendeleev discovered the periodic table, he expressed joy at having discovered the fundamental Reality of the God of the universe.
>
> Without an awakened religious consciousness, it is not possible to delight in such a discovery...
>
> Shortly before he died, Thomas Edison wrote that it is disastrous for a civilization to have science if it lacks religious piety.
>
> Faraday, who invented the electric motor, and Morse, who invented the telegraph, were assisted by their religious convictions to make these discoveries. Millikan, Compton, Carrel, Weyl, and Einstein make their observations of the universe with a religious conscience, approaching the search for truth with humility.
>
> As a result, if Japan's natural sciences are not constructed on religious convictions, they will not contribute to the rebuilding of the nation.[11]

As you will see from the broad range of themes that Kagawa takes up, he took an exceptionally broad view of things in an age that was witnessing increasing specialization. He imagined his own life as a consequence of and participant in a great, unfolding cosmic drama. Kagawa's work is best read as the effort of an artistically gifted religious thinker to constantly step back and mindfully focus

---

11. Kagawa Toyohiko, *Guideposts for New Life* [in Japanese], *Collected Works of Kagawa Toyohiko*, vol. 13, 51.

on the grand production of the entire universe, seeking to "see all things whole."

On a personal note, I was hit by the Kagawa bug rather late in my own career. Upon returning in 2008 from 20 years as a Presbyterian Mission Co-worker assigned to higher education in Japan, I worked for several years at the Center of Theological Inquiry in Princeton. In the fall of 2010, former Princeton Theological Seminary President Iain Torrance invited me to deliver the seminary's Kagawa Memorial Lecture on April 5, 2011. I knew about Kagawa and his contributions as a social reformer. But as I began to wade through the primary and secondary Japanese sources in preparation for my lecture, I came face to face with a truly creative thinker, someone who I think should be honored, with certain critical caveats, as a great Christian mystic and artist. While Kagawa had been marginalized due to the internal church politics touched on above, I became convinced that, in spite of certain undeniable eccentricities and flaws, he needed to be remembered within the company of the great "cloud of witnesses" of the Church.

Since then, I have been trying to understand this extraordinary Japanese Christian in his own context and on his own terms, while beginning to redress the Kagawa amnesia both in Japan and the United States. Thankfully, I have had generous supporters and colleagues in both countries for this emerging new work on Kagawa. Namely, in 2012 the John Templeton Foundation awarded me a three-year research grant that included support for my research on Kagawa, and the Japan International Christian University Foundation in New York City appointed me as a research fellow, welcoming my project as an extension of their own mission to support ICU, an outstanding liberal arts college in Tokyo that rose from the ashes of ww ii. In Japan, Kayama Hisao, Director Emeritus of the Kagawa Archives and Resource Center, welcomed me as a research fellow, and he and his staff have provided prompt and professional support for my ongoing research. Finally, under the leadership of the late

Kagawa Tokuaki, Kagawa's grandson, the staff and associates of the Kagawa Memorial Hall in Kobe warmly welcomed me into their ongoing exploration and conversation on Kagawa's contemporary significance for religious communities and society. The present book is intended to give a new generation of English readers the chance to hear firsthand from one of the most remarkable religious figures of the twentieth century.

We want to refer readers to the following works:

Robert Schildgen: *Toyohiko Kagawa: Apostle of Love and Social Justice* (Centenary, 1988). Referred to as Schildgen.

Thomas John Hastings, *Seeing All Things Whole: The Scientific Mysticism and Art of Kagawa Toyohiko (1888–1960)* (Pickwick, 2015). Referred to as *Seeing All Things Whole.*

Kagawa Toyohiko, *Cosmic Purpose*, Translated by James W. Heisig, Edited by Thomas John Hastings (Cascade, 2014). Referred to as *Cosmic Purpose.*

Mutō Tomio, the editor of Kagawa's collected works, provides important biographical background for these mediations that readers should keep in mind.

The second time Kagawa experienced a loss of vision [caused by the trachoma he had contracted while living in the Shinkawa slum] was on March 21, 1926, and he was hospitalized for forty-four days as the blindness continued until May 17 of the same year. During that time, he dictated these religious meditations to Yamaji Hideo and Yoshimoto Kenko. They were then posted in the religion column of the Yomiuri Newspaper. Since the Yomiuri posts cover two hundred times, it is probable he completed them himself after recovering from the eye ailment.[12]

---

12. Mutō Tomio, "Commentary on *A Few Words in the Dark*," *Collected Works of Kagawa Toyohiko* [in Japanese], vol. 22, 394.

A Few Words in the Dark

Kokoro at the Depth of All Things (3)

At the depth of all things is *kokoro.*[1] Beyond darkness is light. Even though light has been taken from me, still I glimpse a bright radiance.[2] To me, all things speak a poetic word,[3] a deep, affectionate word. The *futon*, tears, saliva, sweat, walls, wet compress, ceiling, *tatami* mat, the cry of the sparrow—all speak a poetic word. God and all inanimate things speak to me.

Even though I have been cast into the darkness, I am not lonely.

1. We have deliberately retained the Japanese word 心 *kokoro* throughout, usually translated as "heart," because it is a multivalent concept encompassing a range of meanings, such as heart, mind, will, emotion, spirit, sense, vitality, etc. My understanding of Kagawa's use of *kokoro* has been enriched by conversation with the creative interdisciplinary scholars at the Kokoro Research Center at Kyoto University; especially Professor Kamata Tōji. Their research focuses on the following three areas: "*kokoro* and body" (mind, brain, and body), "*kokoro* and personal relationships" (emotion, communication, and interaction), and "*kokoro* and lifestyle" (consciousness, values, and life). See http://kokoro.kyoto-u.ac.jp/en/AboutUs/greetings.html.

2. "Bright radiance" is 光明 *kōmei*, a bright light, signifying wisdom or compassion emanating from the Buddha.

3. 詞 *kotoba*, meaning "word" but with a poetic significance, hence our translation "poetic word."

The Miracle of Living (8)

It is a miracle! A miracle! Living is a miracle. Dying is a miracle. Scientific law is a miracle. Reality is a miracle. Falling ill is a miracle. Getting well is a miracle.

Everything exists apart from me. This fact in itself is a miracle. The dragonfly jumps. The hairy caterpillar becomes a butterfly. Fresh leaves sprout. The branches of the oriental elm tree whisper to me. Ants wiggle in the sand. All is miracle!

The world is governed by a power beyond me. Bowing my head, I meditate on the miracle of the unchanging natural world whose form continually evolves.

Confucius (9)

Confucius was a wise person. He figured out how to make use of the whole of life. Even in an age when violence was seen as the final victor, with benevolence, righteousness, decorum, wisdom, and honesty, he proclaimed benevolence as the truly ultimate champion.

I sit on my sick bed and listen to the words of Confucius. He is indeed an extraordinary person. Nevertheless, I still find something lacking. In the end, Confucius is a social man, not a man of solitude. He provides no comfort in my days of sickness. He is simply too wise. Hence, he does not come near the poor, the sick, the least of these.

Mohammed (10)

Mohammed is also very wise. I admire his Koran. He is very solemn. But as a prophet of a dreadful judgment, he does not proclaim a gospel of salvation for the wounded, the troubled, the least of these. Except for the massive Persian silk tree,[4] all other trees wither in the hot winds of the desert. I respect Mohammed, but I cannot imagine him as my comforter.

---

4. 「合歓の木」 *nemunoki*, albizia julibrissin.

The Buddhist Scriptures and Me (11)

Of all of the Buddhist scriptures, the three I like most are the Saddharma Puṇḍarīka Sutra, the Vimalakīrti Sutra, and the Avataṃsaka Sutra. Among these three, my favorite is the Saddharma Puṇḍarīka or Lotus Sutra. The Lotus Sutra teaches me the three great truths of "eternal life," "enlightenment," and "never despising." I know this represents the greatest contribution of Eastern thought. But the world of the Lotus Sutra is a world in tatters. It is as if the soul has lost its critical facility in reaching the highest boiling point.

The world of the Vimalakīrti Sutra is a world of atonement for sin. It is an expression of the great artistry of the Eastern world, or that is the point of view I wish to take. But the Vimalakīrti Sutra does not designate the path of the seeker who finally reaches the domain of atonement for sin. The Lotus Sutra does reveal this path to the seeker. From the Lotus Sutra, I learn that my soul clings to the earth. Some call this philosophy, but I think of it in terms of moral psychology.

I become awakened to the transfiguration of my soul as I ascend the way of the ten stages,[5] one at a time. Let me read the Lotus Sutra freely for a while without making distinctions such as "Buddhist" or "Christian." I am a seeker. I hunger and thirst for the transfiguration of my soul. Plato himself did not penetrate to this depth in his critique of the soul.

---

5. 十地 jūji. "Various sets of ten stages of practice are found in different texts and traditions." *Digital Dictionary of Buddhism*, Online: http://www.buddhism-dict.net/ddb/. (hereafter called *DDB*).

In the darkness, I glimpse the pitiful form of the ascetic of the Lotus Sutra whose body is crushed as it moves toward divine transfiguration.

One Impregnated by God (13)

Yes indeed! It is not so much that I believe in God, it is that God impregnates me. That is why I have had to close my eyes for so long. That is also why I have had to feel such discomfort. I am enwombed, enwombed by God. God must expect something great from us. I must not say I am suffering or I am sad and thereby fall into utter despair. God enwombs me. An uncertain consciousness gives way to feeble effort, which turns to prophesies of things in the next world rather than to the pressing issues at hand.

But we must never allow it! While seeming unconscious, we are not unconscious, while seeming conscious, we are not conscious. The deep life of viviparity[6] for those who dwell on earth is like the baby chick undergoing transformation within the egg. The dawn is yet far off. For the moment, let us clip our wings, gird up our loins, close our eyes, and behold the great holy works of the Majesty on high.

6. Kagawa choses the word 胎生 *taisei*, "viviparity," which in Japanese has both a biological and Buddhist connotation, as follows: "Uterine birth, born from a womb. Or, a being that is born from a womb. One of the four kinds of births 四生 *shishō*. Before the differentiation of the sexes birth is supposed to have been by transformation. The term is also applied to beings enclosed in unopened lotuses in paradise, who have not had faith in Amitābha but trusted to their own strength to attain salvation; there they remain for proportionate periods, happy, but without the presence of the Buddha, or bodhisattvas, or the sacred host, and do not hear their teaching. The condition is known as 胎宮 *taigū*, the womb palace." (*DDB*). For more detail on Kagawa's use of maternal metaphors for God, see discussion in *Seeing All Things Whole*, 164–72.

Salvation and New Life (18)

To me, salvation and regeneration mean the same thing. I believe that the psychological experience of salvation shares the same substance with the regenerative power filling the cosmos. I rely completely on this power. Along with evolution, I believe in ongoing evolution. And I believe the solution to ongoing evolution is the solution of faith.

Let the scoffers scoff! Without this faith I cannot live even a single day. The sicklier my body becomes, the more deeply I must take hold of this faith.

The Christ who does not Propose Theories (21)

The wisdom of Christ is found in the fact that he did not propose theories. Those who prefer theories are better off avoiding Jesus. Essentially, religion is not some theory, it is life. Jesus beheld God without theory. And the God he beheld was the most Godlike of all, because he did not approach God as the philosophers, with concepts such as limitless absolute, omniscient almighty, or universal reality. His God was the remarkably natural Father and the remarkably natural Shepherd. The gentle God was revealed in the gentle Jesus. Only a theoretical God will be revealed to modern people who insist that no thing lacking theory is credible.

Science as Art (22)

To me, science is the perfect art. I have never thought science and religion are in conflict. I want to learn more and more of the depths of science. By so doing, I believe I will understand the cosmos more deeply. And the more deeply I understand the cosmos, the more deeply I will understand myself. And the more deeply I understand myself, the more deeply I will understand God.[7]

Those who claim religion and science are at odds are themselves at odds with science. Are not all things for us? Or rather, are not all things for the God who moves within our innermost selves? The God who moves within is also the God who moves without.

Through my self, I see what emerges in the sciences as art.

7. This view reflects Kagawa's religious personalism, which is also shaped by the older reformed theology; cf. the opening chapter of Calvin's *Institutes* on the paradoxical relation between knowledge of God the creator and knowledge of ourselves.

Nearly all the wisdom we possess, that is to say, true and sound wisdom, consists in two parts: the knowledge of God and the knowledge of ourselves. But, while joined by many bonds, which one precedes and brings forth the other is not easy to discern.

John Calvin, *Institutes of the Christian Religion,* ed. by J. T. McNeill (Philadelphia: Westminster, 1960), I.1.35.

Seeing Religion as the Art of Life (27)

I will say it once again. There is no greater art than religion, though what is commonly called art is just one aspect of art through the senses. Only religion as the art of life pertains to the entire art of living.

By living in religion, I am enabled for the first time to sit before the mirror of God. All *kokoro* bear the pattern of objects as an expression, and all objects reveal the state of the *kokoro*.[8] Religion is a joyful art and, to me, it is the ultimate art. There is no need to be scrutinized by anyone. I walk alone as an object of the divine art. Even when I am alone in the darkness, God diligently watches over me. God and I act together in every drama. Yet even when I utterly fail in my role, God never treats me with contempt.

8. See note 1 above.

No Salvation without Love (28)

Some think of salvation in terms of utility. I do not see it that way. Salvation is the inexhaustible power of the immense love of the cosmos. Without love there is no such thing as salvation. There is salvation only where there is love. The hand of salvation is extended to those lacking love and value. Faith in salvation is to believe that this love is hidden in the innermost depths of the cosmos. Buddhism also recognizes this, hence it is not in the least bit surprising that Christianity discovered this. In God, there is no distinction made between Buddhism and Christianity. There is nothing but this singular love. And within this great plan, God entrusts one part even to someone as insignificant as me. I am truly grateful.

A Holistic Life and Spiritual and Social Movements (30)

Some say social movements and spiritual movements are two separate things. These are people who do not think of religion as the art of the whole life. They are able to say such things by saying spirit and matter are separate things or that God and the world have no relation. However, for those who live according to the *summum bonum*,[9] there can be no distinction between social movements and spiritual movements. Indeed, is it even possible for social movements to exist independently from spiritual movements? Only cowards proclaim a dualism between God and the world.

Real religion does not doubt that God meddles all the way down into the stock exchanges.

9. The "highest good," a notion rooted in Aristotle and taken up for Christian theology by Thomas Aquinas, but also consonant with the Neo-Confucian notion of 致良知 *chiryōchi*. Cf. *Seeing All Things Whole*, 64–74.

Four Meanings of the Void (31)

I see four meanings of the void. These are the four modalities of the "nothing" of the past, the "nothing" of the future, the "nothing" of things that exist, and the "nothing" of things of value.

Many nihilistic youth say a world of nothingness exists. In such a case, this is a nothingness of reality, not a nothingness of nothingness. The nothingness of nihilistic youth is the illusion of a nonexistent world, as in the nonexistence of the past in regards to the present or the sense that the future is still without existence. But true nothingness is nothing other than the nothingness of no value. The absence of value is authentic nothingness, and only those with a soul are able to grasp this. Only those who realize that the power of denial, avulsion, and abandonment exist in the innermost soul know the true meaning of the void. In this sense, the Buddha was a pioneer in observing the soul through the void. Only after denying the sugar-sculpted mundane world could his authentic soul be restored.

Knowledge of God through Love's First Flowering (37)

Before there was an initial budding of love in my innermost soul, I did not understand what is called God's love. To a selfish soul, there is a tendency to think of all blessings as something to be expected. However, once such a person meets with some calamity, they quickly become pessimistic and begin to curse God and the world.

Love is that which is innermost. When we do not begin to take the initiative, we cannot comprehend the preciousness of a person's love. It is like the wealthy who do not know the hardships of the worker. Love is that which is innermost, and such love alone approaches God. Once we seek to live in love, we realize immediately the true form of the cosmos. And that form is love. "Whoever does not love does not know God, for God is love."[10]

---

10. 1 John 4:8.

The Absoluteness of Love (38)

Love knows all things. Love knows what it is to be sad, to laugh, to endure, to move, to be hungry, to grow, to take risks.

Love also knows what it is to show respect, to be proud, or when to be generous. This is because love approaches perfect knowledge.

Love accepts suffering. Love can perform wonders. This is because love approaches perfect power.

Love boils, love permeates. Love melts, love embraces. Thus love approaches the form of free accommodation. Love is the ultimate reality.

The Art of the Soul (40)

Compared with the art of the soul, all other arts are but shadows. While the color painted on a canvas cannot revive a hungry soul, those who apply themselves to the art of the soul make the blind see, the lame walk, and the hungry satisfied. They apply oil to those whose souls are wounded.

This art is the sculpture of life chiseled into body and soul, and one is changed into the form of the cosmos when beholding it.

Courage, integrity, self-denial, tribulation, charity, and resourcefulness are the hammer and chisel utilized in the art of the soul. The art of the soul will never grow weary for all eternity.

Dwelling in the Least of These (42)

Behold, God dwells in the least of these. God dwells in the imprisoned convict sitting on the trash heap. Is God not truly present in the homeless child, in the beggar begging food at the gate, in the patients gathered at the infirmary, in the unemployed standing in line at the free job placement agency? Those who want to meet God do well to first visit the prison before going to the temple. Going to the hospital before going to church. Helping the beggar at the gate before reading the Bible. Might you not miss God if you put off the prison for the temple alone? Will you not miss the chance to worship the image of God if you go to church only and put off going to the hospital? If you get absorbed in reading the Bible without helping the beggar at the gate, I fear you may miss the God who dwells in the least of these. Those who forget about the unemployed forget about God.

Seeing God through a Microscope (46)

I always experience a deep religious feeling when looking through a microscope. When looking at the initial generation of a young chick prepared on a slide and seeking the whereabouts of the x and y chromosomes, observing the Brownian motion of molecules, or when shown the *zona radiata*,[11] or examining the organization of a mineral in a microscope, without reason it is as if I feel that I enter right into the great mysterious world of the cosmos. It seems the astronomer Herschel[12] said that those who observe the cosmos through a telescope and say there is no God are fools, and I wish to apply his words to those who peer through a microscope: "Those who peek through a microscope and cannot grasp the mystery of the cosmos are mad."

11. Membrane next to the yolk of an ovum, which is separated by a very delicate membrane.

12. Frederick William Herschel (1738–1822).

Ant Nests (47)

As a kind of experiment, I had the youngsters in my household make two ant nests. The first was made in a box vertically, and the second was made in a box horizontally. Their first great surprise was to see the ants' kindness toward some other ants that were weary from working. From his mouth, one ant fed a yellow liquid to an exhausted friend who had returned to the nest. Other injured ants were carried back to the nest in order to rest. The world of ants reveals a kindness one cannot depend on in the human world.

Even now I feel disgraced before the ants. Rather than just read about it in a book, to actually demonstrate it, and then to realize how we humans engage in so many worthless activities, I feel compelled to repent before the ants.

Earthquakes, Volcanic Eruptions, and Revolutions (48)

Some people cry that violence appears to be the solution to everything. If violence were so important, would it not be beneficial to welcome earthquakes and volcanic eruptions at any time? If this were the case, such forces would contribute more to the evolution of human society than Newton or Edison.

But militarist parties, dictators, and violent anarchists do not control the evolution of human society. The evolution of human society is increased by motives conceived of in terms of law, selection, effort, invention, and the *summum bonum*.[13]

A world that can be influenced by violence will fall by violence. I am not able to live in such an untrustworthy world.

I have no expectations whatsoever regarding violence in any form. Only the power from within can raise us up. This is the energy of the *summum bonum*, which is science, invention, discovery, art, playwriting, and morality. Apart from these inner forces the power of external things is too weak. I do not trust them.

---

13. See note 9 above.

Transcendence and Incarnation (49)

Takayama Chogyū[14] taught, "By every means, we must
not fail to transcend the present time." To this statement, I
should like to add the following, "Those who know the way of
transcendence must know the way of incarnation." This is the
way to which the *Kegon Sutra*[15] points and the way taken by
the carpenter of Nazareth. In the carpentry of the carpenter's
son scorned by gluttons and drunkards, there was no dream of
separating labor and religion. Neither fasting nor maintaining
the purity rituals, he was friend to sinners and confidant to
prostitutes, thoroughly stained by the dirt of everyday life. That
was the way of his incarnation. As a criminal condemned to
death, he thus took the downhill direction by dying on the cross.
He whose end was a bloodbath of the flesh entered into the final
religion. When the final word of the criminal condemned to die
on the cross was spoken, the world and every last one remaining
in it was drawn into God.

14. 高山 樗牛 (1871–1902), Japanese philosopher famous for his 1902 essay, "On the
Aesthetic Life."

15. Flower Garland Sutra.

The Image of Kannon (52)

I once saw an image of Kannon[16] from the Song Dynasty in China. Still owned by a wealthy person from Kansai, it is truly beautiful. But then I discovered a national difference between the faces of the Chinese and Japanese images of Kannon. The Japanese image of Kannon is extremely intellectual, while the Chinese one is strikingly relaxed. Depending on your point of view, you might say the Chinese image is more generous. But, as for me, regarding which should be the more loveable, I think I would wish people to love the Japanese Kannon. This woman glowing with a wisdom and a love purified by truth—it is exactly through such a power of intensity that the pain of life may be wiped out. I think the Japanese Kannon represents the Japanese woman. May the *kokoro*[17] of Kannon be forever implanted in the women of Japan.

16. Female Buddhist image revered by Asians for mercy and compassion.
17. See note 1 above.

The Blue Cliff Record and the Smile of Life (53)

When I opened the *Blue Cliff Record*,[18] I learned it shows signs of the smile of life. In the last chapter of his *Divina Commedia*, Dante writes, "The universe smiled," but I was taught this ultimate joke in the Eastern world through the *Blue Cliff Record*. Unspoken, unspeakable, and with voice unheard, I learned through the *Blue Cliff Record* that truth, ever smiling, presses in upon us.

It is a wonderful that many Japanese jokes originate in Zen with Zen priests, but I wish to laugh at a slightly higher pitch. In the spirit of Ikkyū,[19] who in his finely embroidered monk's stole was moved to laughter at meaningless religious precepts, I wish to snicker at all of the idols and worthless pretensions to political authority in our own time. In the sound of Dante's laughter, the papal miter falls, and in the jokes of the *Blue Cliff Record*, we see all idols come tumbling down from their jeweled altars in ruins.

18. 「碧巌録」*Hekiganroku*. "A collection of one hundred *gong'an* 公案 (*kōan* in Japanese), originally compiled by the fourth-generation Yunmen 雲門 monk Xuedou Zhongxian 雪竇重顯 (980–1052) and later commented on by the 11th century monk Yuanwu Keqin 圜悟克勤(1063–1135). Considered as an outstanding representative of Chan literary quality, this text became a central object of study for later *kanhua* (看話) practitioners." *DDB*.

19. 「一休宗純」 *Ikkyū Sōjun*, 1394–1481, "Japanese Zen monk of the *Daitokuji* 大德寺 lineage, and is one of the best known Zen monks in Japan for a variety of reasons. He spent much of his middle years pursuing a wandering life-style that resulted in many contacts outside monastic institutions. He wrote works of Zen teaching in vernacular Japanese for a wide audience. Several prominent writers and artists of the late Muromachi period were his disciples." *DDB*.

The Way of the Vimalakīrti Sutra and the Way of Jesus (54)

Bound by the everyday world, we easily become vulgar people accumulating worldly goods, but still the way of the Vimalakīrti Sutra[20] and the way of the carpenter Jesus are practices for keeping our hearts from losing devotion. Whether we are placing our hands in the wash tub, checking under the stove to see if the flame needs stoking with the bamboo blowpipe, repeatedly writing the numbers one through nine in a ledger book, squatting in a rice paddy, being scorched by the sunlight, or standing before a 1600 degree blast furnace, if we cannot live a religious life of prayer as if in a monastery, there will be no salvation for the world. There is no hope for salvation for those who carry their bodies to the mountain while leaving their *kokoro*[21] in the village. And though a weak religion, which cannot save the village, may attain a "geographic" salvation among those who soar the mountain heights, it cannot save the whole person. Mountains and institutions are no substitute for the gospel. True salvation begins from the *kokoro*. If it seems there is no salvation among the masses and in the towns, then the true religion of life has not yet begun.

20. "This scripture is considered one of the most profound, as well as literarily excellent of the Indian Mahāyāna sūtras. The sutra expounds the deeper principle of Mahāyāna as opposed to lesser vehicle teachings, focusing on the explication of the meaning of nonduality. A significant aspect of the scripture is the fact that it is a teaching addressed to high-ranking Buddhist disciples through the mouth of the layman bodhisattva Vimalakīrti, who expounds the doctrine of emptiness in depth, eventually resorting to silence." *DDB*.

21. See note 1 above.

Three Stages in the Evolution of Love (55)

In love there is something unconscious, something subconscious, and something conscious. The evolution of the placenta and the ovary belong to the unconscious, while sexual love, motherly love, mutual love, and love of nation are subconscious.

When taking the form of sacrifice, reparation, and redemptive love that does not withhold death on the cross for the sake of unknown sinners, love finds its final development. In this fully conscious love, the love that seeks to repair the last remaining flaws in the cosmos is born anew. This love, which is the unconscious love within the cosmos, breaks forth as conscious love. This is where I know the cosmic will as love on an unconscious level, love on a subconscious level, and love on a conscious level. This is my philosophy, my science, and my religion.

The Mystery of Weeds (58)

A friend created for me a garden of weeds. In the garden he planted a mixture of around 60 different weed varieties, including *rumex japonicas* (dockweed) that looked like water lilies, something called "double eleven" with countless lavender flowers resembling those of the paulownia tree, the misty *stellaria alsine* (chickweed), and the sun-colored *ranunculus silerifolius* (fox peony).

He cut the tops off of several boxes and wrote the names of each weed in thick letters on cardboard. What surprised me was something I had not noticed previously. Among the weeds were countless flowering plants. Even if not as elegant in appearance as the *cephalanthera falcate* (golden orchid) or the *cephalanthera erecta* (silver orchid), *spiranthes* (ladies' tresses) reminds one of the ruby-studded ceremonial staffs held by Western kings and *alopecurus aequalis* (short-awned foxtail) closely resembles the traditional bearskin helmets worn by the Imperial Guards of the United Kingdom. Think of the amazing energy of *erigeron canadensis* (Canadian horseweed) that has recently come from Canada and conquered all of Japan! When I think carefully about the life of each weed, I recognize the mystery of the cosmos also dwells there.

The Miracle of Myself (59)

I am a miracle. There is no need to make an external inquiry. My physical existence as well as my spiritual existence is a miracle of miracles. It is a wonder I was born in the first place, lonely as a shadow, and while being merely human I have constantly battled many diseases, so my survival itself is a miracle. But the greatest miracle of all is my spiritual existence. Enabled to triumph over temptations, shielded from the world's depravity, and empowered forward on the spiritual path, I can only conclude that I am a miracle of miracles. At times, gusts of evil thoughts have shaken me to my core. Yet when I recall that a double or even ten times stronger and purer power possesses and guides me, such a state of mind makes me think it is all a kind of miracle. To my mind, value immediately becomes reality, and prayer soon takes actualized form. Daily I sense the wonder of imagination deep within me, and the miracle of resurrection is not a thing of the past but it occurs in my heart today. God conceived in the Virgin Birth is not just an old tale of Bethlehem but my present reality.

Transcending Self-Power and Other-Power (60)

Human beings make a distinction between self-power and other-power.[22] But to my mind, everything is both for God and for oneself. There is not a single thing that does not depend on God. And once I realize that God's love works completely to my benefit, I feel that love permeates me as a volcanic eruption. When the eruption penetrates me, the other-power is personally the very thing itself. Thus I do not wish to distinguish between self-power and other-power. Life is something transcendent that is also something immanent. Doing something to benefit another also benefits oneself. Those who work for others must not neglect their own progress. In order for those who help others to bear a twofold burden for another and for one's self, one must not resist exerting the effort of two people. Even if this ability comes from the replenishment of transcendent power, as soon as it springs up in your breast, it also constitutes a self-effort. Once you discover that divine effort is also self-effort, work becomes joy, which means the discovery of the supreme art.

22. It has been commonly asserted that Buddhism is generally a religion centered in 自力 *jiriki* ("self-power") while Christianity is generally a religion centered in 他力 *tariki* ("other-power.") Kagawa, a Christian nurtured in a Buddhist cultural milieu, seeks a way to preserve both aspects, thereby overcoming this duality. Besides the Buddhist and Christian elements here, he is also clearly influenced by Neo-Confucian notions of self-cultivation and spiritual progress.

A History of Misunderstandings (61)

I take no issue with those who say that much of the history
of religious dogma is a history of misunderstandings. But I do
not wish to view these misunderstandings through the cold
eye, for example, of physical chemistry. On the contrary, I want
to treat dogma in light of the insights of psychoanalysis. Most
arbitrary dogma is born out of an emotional logic. Feeling fosters
devotion, devotion gives way to exaggeration, and exaggeration
gives birth to idols, and hence the birth of idols is an outcome of
devotion. But will a day ever come when we will no longer need
feeling? Will there ever be a time when we will have no need for
devotion? Feeling, along with life, has a long history. Compared
to feeling, knowledge is more of a subsequent appendage. And
regardless of how much knowledge seeks to cool the ardor
of passion by pouring cold water on it, or regardless of how
much progress science makes, the élan vital gushes forth and
certain mysterious dogmas with a symbolic significance like the
notation used to denote music will remain forever. Thus, without
abolishing it, our task is to interpret dogma as a sign.

No Need to Define God (62)

When reading a certain book, I discovered something interesting written there. In order to avoid conceptual confusion, the Roman Emperor Constantine, the first ruler to grant freedom to Christianity, convened the world's first religious conference at Nicaea in Asia Minor. On that occasion, certain Christian thinkers were in such a hurry to "define" Christ that they forgot to obey him. The author called this the beginning of the fall of Christianity.

Today there are still many theologians and pastors who think that the essence of Christianity is to define Christ. For this reason there are many religious leaders who look down their noses at those who work themselves to the bone following Christ in the life of service and brotherly love. To such people, defining truth is a higher and more valuable task than liberating the working classes. As a result, such people consider the religion of the lectern to be nobler than the movement for brotherly love. But the religion Jesus taught should be exactly the opposite. Jesus taught the practice of love, not the defining of God.

Cosmology as Art (63)

Cosmology rightly belongs as part of a great artistic movement. Within the world of thought, cosmology makes an ultimate appeal to value. This is why religion is always forgetting the close to hand programs of neighborly love and leaping toward appeals to value, which are upheld by particular cosmologies. Many of the religious wars of the past were battles between invented cosmologies. If people had persisted instead in the close to hand programs of neighborly love, there may have been no religious wars. Today again many vague philosophical constructions (invented cosmologies) have been appropriated by faith, and hence we see so many religious leaders always itching for a fight. Inventors of cosmologies think theirs is the ultimate one. And this is where quarrels arise. Of course, I do not want to say all cosmologies are evil. Some have sufficient artistic weight. Yet I do not wish to waste a single precious life on the relative merits of fictional cosmologies.

Does Light Come from the East? (64)

It is a fashion to say light comes from the East. And some even seem to say the true light is in the East. But light knows no East and no West. Even if the sun rises in the east, the light illuminating the *kokoro*[23] has no geographical existence. The truth is that light comes from the *kokoro*. We cannot allocate it geographically by saying the light is India or the light is Japan. In the South Seas or in the Western nations, light surges forth everywhere, illuminating the springs of the *kokoro*. Since the Western nations have become captive to the machine civilization and forgotten the movement for human love, the saying that light comes from the East has become fashionable. But in that case, where in the East has human love been perfectly realized? Just because Gandhi alone proclaims non-violent love does not mean light is shining from the East. There is no light apart from human love. In light, truth, and spirit, there is no relation of north, south, east, or west. When we are captive to geographical relations, light will not shine in our hearts.

23. See note 1 above.

Zen Priests and the Simple Life (66)

Among the many lifestyles in Japan, the one I love most is that of the Zen priest. I often think how, if only it were a little more productive, it would be very pleasant indeed. Awakened by the stars at dawn, falling asleep with the twilight of evening, eating a vegetarian diet to one's heart's content, mindless of one's finely embroidered black robes, worshipping at the temple, eating rice gruel, meditating, and breaking through to the world of intuition. There are good reasons why the lifestyle of the priest became a kind of norm for daily life after the Ashikaga.[24] However, if we think about what it lacked in its influence on daily life in Japan, it tended toward seclusion from the world, lacking an air of enterprise, adventure, and freedom. In spite of such weaknesses, I constantly give thanks for its conscientiousness, simplicity, non-attachment, and love of nature.

24. The Ashikaga Shogunate that ruled Japan from 1336 to 1573.

Together with God in the Driver's Seat (67)

A young woman came to visit me. She told me that after graduating from a girl's school, she had studied sewing Western clothes for two and a half years. Finding herself in agony over her busy work schedule, she told me she had decided to become a bus conductor this year just after the New Year. She told me that her former life, with such long working hours as to make her dizzy, had seriously and painfully disturbed her ability to think.

Wiping her tears on her woolen kimono, she said, "Because my position was so prestigious, my thought process changed to such an extent that I became obsessed with the fear that in the next moment I might bungle things." Hearing of her heroic decision and courage and how her exhaustion had led to such a change in her thinking, I thought of my own situation in light of hers and started to cry in sympathy.[25] I listened in sadness as she went on, saying, "Since becoming a bus conductor, out of embarrassment I have not gone anywhere, either to visit my relatives or to church."

Oh my brave daughter! Though your relatives might show contempt for your job and the church may cast you out, never forget that God is standing beside you in the driver's seat!

---

25. Kagawa was notoriously busy, rushing from one speaking engagement, evangelistic meeting, or negotiation to another, in order to support a growing number of projects and co-workers.

Good People and Courage (69)

A burglar has courage. Not fearing the police, he overcomes every obstacle aiming for the right moment and steals into a person's home. Moreover, he works at night while people sleep and does not find sleepless nights at all disagreeable.

Villains have this sense of courage, adventure, and diligence. If good people do not exceed the villain's sense of ardor, adventure, courage, and diligence, we should not expect things in the world to improve. When we look at so-called good people in society, many are timid, many withdrawn and passive. On the other hand, the world calls those hermits who idle their lives away in the forest or mountain saints. What an utter contradiction! In this way, villains increasingly flourish while good people become more and more timid. We must persist to the end in sending right into the midst of the secular world good people rich with a sense of adventure and saints burning with ardor.

Criminals (70)

Most criminals I have observed suffer some pathology. Along with bearing some physical or psychological abnormality, there is inevitably some aberration in the society in which they were brought up. They are cursed either by genetics, malnutrition, family, the slum, or society. I want to reconstruct today's prisons as hospitals. But today's accursed society itself must also be admitted to this hospital. Today's society is a patient suffering from the mental disorder of *dementia praecox*.[26] While this ailment is not easily diagnosed until adolescence, its pathology is now well understood. Are not the banks, military, tobacconists, liquor stores, red light districts, geisha houses, and newspapers all showing symptoms of *dementia praecox*? Like a madman inflicting self-harm, today's society is itself taking on a criminal tendency. Only God or the hospital of God can cure this disease.

26. "The first modern attempt to identify individual psychiatric disorders was made by German scientist Emil Kraepelin, who distinguished two of the most severe mental illnesses: schizophrenia, which he called *dementia praecox*, and manic-depressive illness, which is now known as bipolar disorder."

OED Online, http://yeshebi.ptsem.edu:2088/view/Entry/49639?redirectedFrom=dementia+praecox#eid, accessed April 19, 2015.

Kagawa was extraordinarily sensitized to the negative side effects of Japan's rapid modernization. According to historian Kano Masanao, this transition from Meiji to Taishō was characterized by the huge problems and changes that came about as the nation "unavoidably harvested the immature fruit" of its successes. The slogan of the time was "change," and Kano comments in regard to Kagawa's bestselling novel *Across the Deathline*, "Both in terms of its title and style, this book symbolizes the turning point from late Meiji to Taishō." *Undercurrent of Taishō Democracy*, 12, 15. Kano references from Kanai Shinji, "The Practical Christian Ethos in Kagawa Toyohiko," [in Japanese], Kagawa Archives, ed., *Kagawa Toyohiko in Japanese Christian History*, 135.

Let the Earthquakes Come! (71)

Why do the Japanese people lack an innovative spirit? It is said that almost one million Koreans have migrated to Manchuria since the Japanese annexation of Korea.[27] The northernmost island of Hokkaido only has a population of two million five hundred thousand, but Japanese do not migrate there. Since all of the *omikoshi* (portable shrines) at Japanese Shinto shrines have special places were they are lodged during festivals, I do not understand why the descendants of these gods cannot establish new places to dwell.

What weak-mindedness and lack of courage! This is due to a lack of an innovative spirit. Perhaps the climate in Japan is too warm. In order to become more international, the Japanese will likely have to undergo further hardships. Let an additional two or three huge earthquakes come and shake us! Except for the divine rod, it seems this people will never come to their senses.[28]

27. Following its victory in the Russo-Japanese War, Japan forced Korea into an arrangement called the "Eulsa Treaty," making Korea a protectorate of the Japanese Empire. The word "annexation" is a euphemism for what should be characterized as "colonization."

28. To place these somewhat harsh-sounding comments in context, I suggest you read them with selections 72 and 73 below. Kagawa and his co-workers had helped lead relief efforts in Tokyo following the 1923 Great Kanto Earthquake. Faced with this devastation, he offers his most mature reflections on suffering and Christian faith in the Preface to *Attitudes Toward Suffering* (1923). Cf. *Seeing All Things Whole*, 79–82.

The Great Table that has been Prepared (72)

Having been redeemed by such a great love, I must continue to live a redemptive life. Reconciled to a life of suffering,[29] shuddering at the many adventures before me, I must continue to make progress in bearing the cross for others. Perhaps this is a fate to be lamented. Modern people might indeed laugh at a life so far removed from present day realities. But be that as it may, I want to continue to advance and sit before the great table of suffering that has been prepared for me. From that narrow, cramped seat, I want to silently witness the progress of the great redemptive love of God on earth. In my breast, I can hear the heartbeat of God directly. The deeply hidden and loving purpose of God lifts up those who have fallen, comforts the sorrowing and heals the sick, forgives even sinners, liberates the oppressed, and purifies the hearts of all who are corrupt and vulgar, granting to all the same blessed destiny.

---

29. Kagawa's understanding of the relation between divine agency and human suffering is nuanced by the Buddhist logic in which he was raised. In the Four Noble Truths of Buddhism, suffering is first of all understood as an inevitable aspect of conscious life, which is bound up and distracted by various temporal attachments. The ethical challenge for Buddhists is to seek out the roots of suffering and develop effective means to end suffering. For Kagawa, the cross of Jesus Christ is the divine means for communicating the purpose of suffering and achieving its ultimate cessation in the Kingdom of God. But he also sees the divine gift as the primary motivation for Christian ethical life, which is characterized by bearing the cross on behalf of those who have fallen, the sorrowful, the sick, the sinner, the oppressed, the corrupt, and the vulgar.

Something more Fearful than Earthquakes (73)

What is the 10 billion yen in wealth lost in the earthquake?
In one year the Japanese drink up 1.5 billion yen in alcohol and
spend more than 1 billion on self-indulgent pleasures.[30] The
amount spent on sugar for pastries is no less than 600 million.
The annual cost for tobacco exceeds more than 250 million
yen. If we had a four-year moratorium on alcohol, debauchery,
pastries, and tobacco, wouldn't we more than make up for
the spending on the Great Kanto Earthquake by the Tokyo
municipal government and its six surrounding prefectures?
Therefore I say, instead of the instabilities in the earth's crust,
we should fear the slackness of the ties that bind our souls.[31]
Three years after the earthquake, Japan has completely forgotten.
I am afraid that in the Ministry of Reconstruction there are
government officials who take bribes, in the political parties there
are members of parliament who run off to brothels, and several
prefectures are still wrapped up in scandals. With the nation as a
whole in such a state of moral decay, will even the revelations of
the righteous prevail? May the first day of Spring come quickly!
Completely blow away the decadence of this beloved nation!

30. A reference to prostitution, a well-established institution that exploited young
girls from poor families. Kagawa and his wife Haru, along with many Japanese Chris-
tians and others, fought hard to abolish this system. Since wives and daughters who
lacked basic human rights and legal protections had to bear the wrath of abusive fathers
and husbands, it is no surprise that the temperance movement was linked seamlessly to
the movement to abolish legalized prostitution.

31. The image Kagawa uses here is of the hoops that bind together the staves of a
barrel or cask for storing aging sake, miso, or soy sauce. If the hoops are slackened, the
liquid will drain out.

Oh Melancholy, Melancholy! (74)

Oh Melancholy, melancholy—I seek consolation but this melancholy will not be consoled, I seek to overcome but this melancholy will not be overcome—why must I stare into your face again after such a long time? I have spent half of my almost forty years before your pallid face. Yet you have not abandoned me. My soul trembles before your two shadowy eyes. Bewitched by your gaze, it seems I cannot escape. Enthralled by love's destiny, I cower before your face. Like the cross of Jesus of Nazareth that fell on the shoulders of Simon of Cyrene,[32] I will continue to bear the cross of melancholy as my companion on the way to new life. I hear the voices of the worldly crowd laughing me to scorn. Yet I know that you do not cast me away. Hence, though I cannot lift my head, I hurry through the back streets to Calvary. Oh melancholy, melancholy. Sacred destiny, melancholy.[33]

32. Reference to Mark 15:21:

> They compelled a passer-by, who was coming in from the country, to carry his cross; it was Simon of Cyrene, the father of Alexander and Rufus.

33. This passage indicates that the depression Kagawa had suffered as a youth continued to plague him from time to time into adulthood. See *Seeing All Things Whole*, Chapter 1.

The Art of Suffering (75)

To those who know God, suffering is the greatest art. God sows tears on earth to enrich the substance of our lives. Those devotees who will pay the entrance fee of five yen to see a third rate version of the tragedy of the *Chūshingura*,[34] which makes them weep, need to consider the meaning of the fact that God, free of charge, allows us to view many tragedies on earth. To those seeking to live by their own strength, suffering is an enigmatic trial. It is said that lions drop their three-day old cubs from a cliff. Those born of God must be as strong as God. Are not suffering, disaster, poverty, and persecution akin to the many jewels adorning the crown of life? I will proclaim to my soul, "Let avalanche, tornado, typhoon all come at once! I will not be afraid in the earthquake or in the landslide. For to me, suffering is the ultimate art."

34. Performance based on the popular tale of the Forty-seven Rōnin.

Suffocation from a Religion of Sensation (77)

If one does not live a religion that encompasses the whole life, religion will always fall into corruption. The religion of sensation builds temples, burns incense, presents offerings, worships idols, and beats meaningless gongs, thereby suffocating life. Even when it does not do such things, it becomes fossilized within certain sacred texts, conducting funerals for the dead, enthralled by divinations, creating traditional systems, and before you know it makes superstitions that see pastors, priests, and monks as the sole messengers of God who exploit the masses of parasites who have no awareness they are becoming parasites. A religion of the whole life discovers God in work and in service. Not limiting the holy only to reading scripture and prayer, one sees all of life as holy. Life itself becomes an offering of incense, and work a prayer to God. One's bed is a gracious seat on the altar, one's workplace an extension of the sanctuary. As long as priests, monks, and pastors are viewed as holy, there will be no religion of the whole life on earth.

The Current of Faith (79)

Faith is always flowing in currents. From Mount Hiei
have sprung the three Buddhist faiths of Pure Land, Shin,
and Nichiren. Regardless of how small the tiny seed of faith,
it later becomes as a great tree where the birds may dwell.
During the 13th century in south-west Germany a movement
of the brethren association began in complete anonymity, and
around the time of the Reformation became part of the great
Anabaptist movement, with one branch remaining in Bohemia
becoming the source of the great Herrnhut *unitas fratrum*.[35]
The communal life of one hundred Herrnhut families took two
centuries to reach all of Germany and the formation of its first
foreign mission took only twenty years, which was the occasion
for Wesley's call and the inauguration of England's Methodist
movement, giving a religious foundation to the English labor
unions. These in turn brought forth the Salvation Army, and is
still a great flowing current that cannot be exhausted.

35. Known in English as the Moravian Church.

Before Arguing for the Imperfection of the Cosmos (80)

In order to argue for the imperfection of the cosmos, we must exclude human imagination. If there are such imperfections that the universe cannot mend, they have to do with only one aspect of the universe, yet why does a picture of perfection appear to human imagination? If through human imagination some imperfections in the universe may be mended, we probably should not conclude that the whole universe is imperfect. That is because human imagination itself is surely a product of the cosmic will.[36] I cannot help thinking it is absurd that people who curse the universe commit the fallacy of placing human imagination outside of the universe. I even think that the mirror of perfection in human imagination is conceived within the universe as a perfect mirror, and the universe creates the human and confers consciousness. Those who claim the cosmos has no consciousness are those who wish to make human consciousness an exception to the universe. I have no idea to what extent it may or may not be beneficial to separate the cosmos and human consciousness. I do believe that the human *kokoro*[37] is open to the *kokoro* of the cosmos. Consequently, those who do not despair with regard to themselves have no need of despairing with regard to the cosmos.

36. Since he is addressing mostly non-Christian readers, Kagawa choses neutral or indirect terms such as "cosmic will" or "cosmic life" to refer to God.

37. See note 1 above.

Limits to Mystery (81)

I am opposed to setting limits to the mysterious and pursuing things through the senses alone. For me, reason, law, and even the discovery of mechanism belong to the realm of mystery. I believe that nothing has done so much to lay bare the world of mystery as modern science. The reason science has lost its sense of mystery is because it is disconnected from life. Once we realize life inspires science, it will be clear that mechanism, law, and reason are all supporters of life and thus windows opening into the world of mystery. I am a scientific mystic. The more scientific I am, the more deeply I feel I am breaking into the divine realm. Especially in the field of biology do I feel as though I am participating in a direct interview with God. Through life, I discover purpose even in the sphere of mechanism. Science is the mystery of mysteries. It is the divine revelation of revelations.

Life as Revelation (82)

It is said that revelation is truth entering the substance of our lives. When truth does not control life, perception and life are divided and God and the person exist at a distance from each other. Once truth breaks into one's way of living, God becomes the dynamic force and guiding spirit of daily life. That is why those seeking divine revelation will not meet God, even if they study philosophical epistemology. It must begin by participating in the movement for the creation of values. Those who labor in releasing the oppressed, feeding the hungry, or making the blind see and the poor rich are able to see divine revelation daily. This is really the case. A liberator sees God daily. God speaks personally to him and he bows reverently before God, and while the religious scholar in his study seeks divine revelation in epistemology, the God of life is revealed within personal life. Divine revelation is still not closed. Pseudo-scholars and religionists spurn this truth.

"I" as a Result of History (83)

"I" am a result of the whole of history. This idea is neither old nor new. Those who doubt it are of course free to do so. Actually, if the past history had been so full of glory, one might expect I would be slightly grander. I will repeat myself. As H. G. Wells has written, from the first nebula to the modern age, the history of world culture has its conclusion in the depths of my soul. The history of the world is nothing more and nothing less than me. And through my effort, the subsequent history of the world may progress one further step. Herein lies the attitude that transcends history. I transcend history by progressing one step forward. I must become eternally young. All of the rest of history is an umbilical cord. When the umbilical cord is cut, human beings can see sunlight for the first time. I am in a hurry to transcend history by moving one step forward.

The First Page in my Study of Science (86)

I like to begin my study of science from things in my ordinary environment. I want to know the properties of the soil on which I stand. I want to know about the origins of the fault lines engraved upon the pebbles. I want to be taught the details of the life of the weeds growing by the roadside. I want to know everything there is to know about the stars shining over my head.

Why don't our universities today teach in a little more depth about soil, weeds, and stars? As for natural science, it merely teaches abstractions, while teaching nothing whatsoever about things appearing much closer to hand in our limited world. But what I wish to know about is not a view of things far removed from the ordinary. I want to know about the development of the materials revealed in soil and pebbles. Without a doubt, in the courses of the rings carved onto the surface of pebbles is the parallel development of the ancient history of the earth. I want to know about that. No doubt there is a trace of mystery beyond human knowing hidden in the "wilderness chrysanthemum" that grows abundantly in the desert. What a pity to have lived several decades and still not know the names of the stars we see every night. Oh, I want to know about ordinary things. The ordinary belonging to the ordinary, I want to know about every phenomenon within my environment.

I long for soil, tree, fire, metal, water, and the spirit of the wind to whisper to me!

What is Revealed by the Secret of Water (87)

Those who love water cannot look at its surface only. Its
secret is revealed only to those who actually slip down into the
water. I have seen many of the world's oceans and could not
see much difference by looking at the water's surface alone.
One would not expect the waves of the Pacific and the Atlantic
Oceans to be very different. If we want to know the oceans, we
cannot avoid going deep. Under the sea, completely hidden from
the human race, is a mysterious realm of the enlightened.[38]

I cannot forget the mysterious recollection of pulling up
Chinese lantern plants (*physalis alkekengi*) from the bottom
of the ocean floor under a pier in Kobe Harbor when I was a
child. At the bottom of the perfectly clear saltwater were various
colored seaweeds swaying to and fro like ribbons attached to
the waists of dancing girls. There was a black porgy with its eyes
staring as if it were about to come right at me. Then a speeding
school of striped sea bream crossed right before my eyes.
Crouching in the shadow of a rock was a sepia-colored octopus.
Near the beautiful clinging green *nori*[39] was an uncountable
multitude of Chinese lantern plants with red roots. I would swim
to the bottom like a merman, gather a bunch of the Chinese
lantern plants, and then resurface to catch my breath. I will never
forget the old days when, as a boy in Naruto in Awa, sometimes I
would go to the nearby Ōmiko coast beyond the Komatsushima
Harbor, and dive into the sea to collect turban shell mollusks.

38. Kagawa uses the Buddhist word 聖境 *shōkyō* here. "Basic Meaning: realm of the
enlightened. Senses: Field of the sages (Skt. *ārya-gocara*)." DDB.

39. Seaweed, which when dried, is used to wrap rice in sushi rolls (i.e., *norimaki*).

It was after these kinds of experiences of being charmed by the beauty at the bottom of the sea that I became a child of mystery.

The Glory of Incarnation (89)

I am simply incapable of seeing incarnation as something unclean. Ancient peoples saw sensuality as a sin, as if thinking the duty of religion was to be detached from the sensual world. I see sensuality as a supreme delight. Those who live the most ethical and disciplined lives cannot understand why sensuality is viewed as a sin. Sensuality is the wellspring of life and an opening to the ascent to delight.[40] Eating, sleeping, giving birth, and raising children—all are various kinds of pleasure. For those who draw from the wellspring of holy love, marriage and death make the most pleasurable, unceasing music. Embrace is divine melody, bereavement a silent interval in the music. For me, embrace and bereavement together are gracious gifts of God for which I am grateful. Everything is holy and seasoned with love. Only one thing destroys the sacredness of sensuality. That is a sensuality detached from God, and lacking the desire to be purified, a degenerate sensuality that is tormented by the fires of hell.

40. Kagawa uses the word 登山口 *tozanguchi* here, meaning the "starting point of a mountain ascent or trailhead." This view that celebrates sensual desire and its ethical and disciplined expression in marriage is in sharp contrast to the depreciation of bodily appetites in certain religious traditions. Kagawa's robust sexual ethic sounds surprisingly contemporary.

The Invisible Horse (90)

My three year-old boy has a horse that will not eat fodder. Neither my wife nor I have seen this horse. Yet our son believes without doubt that this horse is tethered to a pine tree in front of our shed each morning and evening. Because our son believes so firmly, my wife and I have also come to believe in the existence of that horse. Every day our son mounts the horse and sets out to play among the rows of cherry trees. And he returns home riding his horse. I was delighted that the invisible horse that did not eat fodder became part of our family. Anytime our son spoke with me about the horse, he cheerfully shared stories about the horse's activities.

Our son has no need whatsoever to worry about poverty, since he is always satisfied with an invisible horse, an invisible automobile, or an invisible treasure. His father and mother have been led by this child to touch the joy of the invisible world.

Gratitude for the Changes of the Four Seasons (91)

Whenever traveling in the tropics, I always have the following thought. With animals and plants propagating as if the limitations of the natural world had been completely removed, life there is abundant and pleasant for those who love a natural lifestyle.

Nevertheless, after being there for only three to five days, somehow I feel increasingly bored with the monotonous climate and the hues of deep green trees that never die, and I begin to long for the world of the frigid zone where flying snow pierces the skin. Even if not to such an extreme, I feel it is better to have grown up with four seasons where buds emerge in spring and leaves turn color in fall, and in my heart I long for the temperate zone. Because of this, I said to my soul, "Instead of the overly blessed tropics, I would rather dwell in a country with four seasons that is not so fortunate. Rather than a world where one loses interest in eating, I want to live in a free and changeable country where the whisper of love penetrates suffering."

Religion and Philosophy (92)

My wife's friend heard a university student, whose father is
a Buddhist priest, say, "Christianity is a religion and Buddhism
is a philosophy." She asked me, "Is this true?" It is probable this
student thinks of philosophy as something of higher value than
religion. But I cannot believe that the Buddha rejected religion
and lived a philosophy. No, was it not just the opposite? Denying
all philosophies and complicated worldviews, did he not intend
to make progress toward value on the path of abandonment? The
path walked by the sage Socrates denied a world where imaginary
idols reign. This is a common point between the Buddha and
Socrates. They denied every empty view of the universe and
devoted themselves to the advance of human values. Theirs
were indeed philosophies, but philosophies that gave first place
to ethical intuition and not cosmology. Is not the reason the
Buddha's teachings have persisted until today because religion is
truly about making progress in human values, and specifically
about communicating the deepest art concerning progress in
values? Will there ever come a time when a philosophical view
of the universe will be employed as a substitute for a religion
of ethical progress in values? Cosmology will forever be a
postscript to the ethical invocation of life. Religion is forever
young, philosophy always underdeveloped. To think religion will
disappear before philosophy or that a philosophical view of the
universe is alone adequate is like saying we have no need to eat.

Idols and the Split in the Soul (95)

Idols are generated by a divided soul. Idols are nothing more than photographs of the soul. Through a divided soul, they imagine a dualism between good and evil and believe there are two gods in the cosmos. Those who judge spiritual power as worthless and the external energy of all things as absolute are quick to change all phenomena in the natural world into idols. The number of idols enlarges in proportion to the weakness of the soul. By contrast, those who seek to penetrate the cosmos through the conscience are certain there cannot be more than one God in the universe. Were two gods to exist in the universe, they would not be able to appear as a single *kokoro*[41] in the microcosm of human conscience. For those who believe in a single conscience, there is also one God. Those who believe in the nonexistence of the inner power of conscience claim there is no God in the universe. Human vision is the vision of God, and the human *kokoro* a sanctuary where God dwells. God forsakes those who destroy the sanctuary of the *kokoro*. But atheists actually dwell in close proximity to polytheists. That is to say, at times when fears, tremors, and disasters linger, and the thirst of the tongues of the godless and soulless will not be quenched, atheists, like polytheists, soon begin to believe on their own in the existence of cruel, evil spirits.

---

41. See note 1 above.

Dharma Showers (96)

I am provided with Dharma[42] showers[43] from heaven and
deep pleasure from the marrow of my soul. Staring at the wall,
seated in *seiza* (silent meditation), a supremely comforting
religious ecstasy presses in upon me. Moment by moment I
can taste the divine nectar flowing from the wellspring of life.
The walls, the tatami mats, the charcoal burner, and even my
much-afflicted body are in the gentle palm of God's hand. Held
in God's gentle hand, the crimson arteries of God warm my
paralyzed heart. Divine love is stronger than that of a human
lover. Divine light[44] is my nourishment, holy cleansing the
very air I breathe. Even though I cannot see God's face, I see
the touch of God's fingertips before me always. Even when the
scribbling of God's fingertips is ordinary, it is yet more beautiful
than the sky at dawn. While I have not witnessed the creation of
heaven and earth, as one firmly embraced in the palm of God's

42. "Rendered into English variously according to the context as: truth, reality; phenomenon, element, constituent, (mental) factor; things, quality (Tib. *chos*;
Pāli dhamma). The word dharma is originally derived from the Indic root *dhr*, with
the meaning of 'that which preserves or maintains,' especially that which preserves or
maintains human activity. The term has a wide range of meanings in Buddhism, but
the foremost meaning is that of the teaching delivered by the Buddha, which is fully
accordant with reality. Thus, truth, reality, true principle, law (Skt. *satya*; Tib. *chos*). It
connotes Buddhism as the perfect religion. The Dharma is also the second component
among the Three Treasures (*triratna*) 佛法僧 *buppōsō* (the Buddha, the dharma, and the
saṃgha), and in the sense of dharmakāya 法身 *hōshin* (Dharma-body) it approaches the
Western idea of 'spiritual'." [Charles Muller; source(s): Soothill, Hirakawa, YBh-Ind,
M-W JEBD, Yokoi, Iwanami]." *DDB*.

43. "The rain of Buddha-truth which fertilizes all beings. Buddhist teachings dis-
pensed freely and indiscriminately to all living beings, like the rain, which falls indiscriminately on and sustains all forms of plant life." *DDB*.

44. Again, Kagawa uses 光明 *kōmei* here, a bright light, signifying wisdom or
compassion emanating from the Buddha or God.

hand, I understand every event occurring in heaven or on earth is a fountain of delight for we who are human.

Daughters of Japan, Do not Scoff at Idol Worshippers! (97)

Daughters of Japan, you must not scoff at your mothers for worshipping idols! Atone for your mothers, since beyond love there is no more potent way to destroy idols. Love elevates all and softens all. Every thing yields to love. Those who would teach love must first love. You must not laugh at your mother's worship of idols before you have loved her. Unseen things, oneness, and salvation are predicated on love, thus for the sake of this divine teaching, cease your sneering and theorizing and first serve your mothers with gentleness. Is not the disposition that serves a mother the greatest offering to God? I never once received any encouragement in faith from my stepmother.[45] Yet I never once went against her wishes. My stepmother followed me into the slum, and of her own free will tenderly received the forgiveness of the cross.[46] Love is the secret of religion and the final dogma.

45. When Kagawa was four years old, his birth mother—his father's concubine—died just a few months after his father had died. Kagawa was then sent to live at the Kagawa homestead with his father's legal wife, the stepmother referred to here. It is little wonder she did not properly nurture the boy.

46. This is a reference to her baptism by Kagawa. See *Seeing All Things Whole*, 20.

Jar Filled with the Oil of Grace, Gush Forth! (98)

Gush forth, gush forth, never exhausted jar filled with the oil of grace, gush forth! When I peek through my tears and lose the radiant light,[47] and the jar of oil is empty and completely dried up, oh gush forth, gush forth, Elijah's jar of oil, gush forth! Though bereft of funds and lacking investments, the divine oil from my jar wells up to overflowing. Just this month when I thought I had reached the end of my tether, once again the oil rose up from the depths. Just as the wondrous heavenly food came down in the wilderness of Sinai to save the multitude of liberated slaves, so the wondrous food comes down from heaven upon me. Laid out on my sickbed, unable to do anything remotely resembling real work, the ravens that delivered food to the prophet Elijah in the wilderness do not abandon me now. Well up, well up, oh fountain of grace! While I may not see the face of God, I see the hand of God every day. Is it not entirely the hand of God who makes just the right amount of oil appear each and every day?

---

47. Again, Kagawa uses 光明 *kōmei* here, a bright light, signifying wisdom or compassion emanating from the Buddha or God.

Only one God for only one Soul (99)

I walk a straight line. I have but one small soul. And I offer this one soul to one God. One love gives birth to one faith, and one faith produces one hope.[48] Neither turning to the right nor to the left, I move along one trajectory alone. It is fine for wise ones to depart from the path. As a fool for God, I will be bound by the way of God.[49] The wise of the world follow two paths or many paths. I have but one path—the path that leads to God. This path joins the two points—God and me—in one straight line. There is no other way for me. Circles or ellipses have no

48. Cf. Eph. 4:4–6

> There is one body and one Spirit, just as you were called to the one hope of your calling, one Lord, one faith, one baptism, one God and Father of all, who is above all and through all and in all.

49. Cf. 1 Cor 1: 18–31.

> For the message about the cross is foolishness to those who are perishing, but to us who are being saved it is the power of God. For it is written, 'I will destroy the wisdom of the wise, and the discernment of the discerning I will thwart.' Where is the one who is wise? Where is the scribe? Where is the debater of this age? Has not God made foolish the wisdom of the world? For since, in the wisdom of God, the world did not know God through wisdom, God decided, through the foolishness of our proclamation, to save those who believe. For Jews demand signs and Greeks desire wisdom, but we proclaim Christ crucified, a stumbling block to Jews and foolishness to Gentiles, but to those who are the called, both Jews and Greeks, Christ the power of God and the wisdom of God. For God's foolishness is wiser than human wisdom, and God's weakness is stronger than human strength. Consider your own call, brothers and sisters: not many of you were wise by human standards, not many were powerful, not many were of noble birth. But God chose what is foolish in the world to shame the wise; God chose what is weak in the world to shame the strong; God chose what is low and despised in the world, things that are not, to reduce to nothing things that are, so that no one might boast in the presence of God. He is the source of your life in Christ Jesus, who became for us wisdom from God, and righteousness and sanctification and redemption, in order that, as it is written, "Let the one who boasts, boast in the Lord."

relation to me. As God's fool, I will forever take the path that joins these two points in one line.

Christ's Fool (100)

Christ's fool! A laughingstock of the world! Truly this is what I am. I have lived half of my 39 years up until now as a fool for Christ. I have left behind the so-called pleasures of the world, and never even seeing a single motion picture, I have spent half of my life in close proximity to garbage heaps. As one who is narrow-minded, scorned, and stubborn, half of my life has been spent counting each passing day in tears. Summoned from the ways of debauchery to stand at the foot of the cross, I am joined to the tiny crowd of the hypocritical and unpatriotic followers of a foreign faith.[50] Still this group does not necessarily welcome me either. Being seen as too serious and uninteresting, I am ostracized as a heretic, socialist, and the son of a prostitute. But such matters are inconsequential, for Christ has taken hold of me.[51] I am a slave of the cross. I am the world's fool. To put it in other words, I am ascending the hill toward holiness, forsaking every worldly thing, standing out like a completely naked man. It is unavoidable that others would see me as ridiculous.

50. The words "foreign faith", of course, is a reference to the tiny Christian movement in Japan, which has never reached a critical mass. Today, about 1% of the Japanese call themselves Christian, yet because of the influence of Christian schools and other public institutions, there are indications that many more feel a close affinity to Christianity even though they do not affiliate with a church through baptism.

51. The phrase "for Christ has taken hold of me" is a quote from Philippians 3:12:
Not that I have already obtained this or have already reached the goal; but I press on to make it my own, because *Christ Jesus has made me his own.*

Religious Inquisitions (101)

Christ was killed by a religious inquisition. The Brahman elders ridiculed the Buddha. It is always the parasites of power and money or the so-called guardians of order who destroy newly germinating movements of conscience. They manufacture their own forms of justice and, in the name of God, crush the people. Yet it is precisely God who is the greatest annoyance to these agendas. The Jewish people were not Christ's only consideration, and the collapse of the royal castle of Kapila was not an issue for the Buddha. With regard to hypocrisy, truth is treasonous. Just as one would expect, Christ was executed on the cross as a child of insurrection, and Socrates made to drink the poison cup as a traitor to the nation. Those who fail to foster conscience and suppress truth through the exercise of power take the fastest path to the destruction of a nation. Spain's collapse attended the Inquisition and Italy declined with the papal government. Before making religious laws, let us first teach the living God dwelling in the depth of conscience. We must not fear truths that are treacherous in regard to hypocrisy. For hypocrisy and not truth destroys nations. Any disorder that arises through the truth is always for the creation of a new order in the coming age.

The Joy of Walking Stark Naked (102)

Nothing is as pleasant as walking through this world stark naked.[52] The more we possess, the more we worry about being robbed, and the more we dress up, the more we worry about soiling our clothing. If our position is high, we worry about falling, and if we boast of great knowledge, we are infuriated when derided. Walk naked. Yes, naked! If we are always ready to be stuffed feet first into a coffin, there will be no regrets when we finally take leave of this world. If we apply ourselves to our task as if already dead, there will surely be at least one great mission for us to accomplish. I always set about my work as if I had already committed suicide. Those who are dead have already escaped death, so whatever subsequent time remains is icing on the cake. To those who have killed themselves, status, fame, and fortune are of no more use than a single strand of twine. As those who have been saved after throwing themselves—just as they are—into the water, if we then determine to walk through

---

52. This may be read as a meditation on dying to self with Christ in baptism, as in Romans 6:1–11:

> What then are we to say? Should we continue in sin in order that grace may abound? By no means! How can we who died to sin go on living in it? Do you not know that all of us who have been baptized into Christ Jesus were baptized into his death? Therefore we have been buried with him by baptism into death, so that, just as Christ was raised from the dead by the glory of the Father, so we too might walk in newness of life. For if we have been united with him in a death like his, we will certainly be united with him in a resurrection like his. We know that our old self was crucified with him so that the body of sin might be destroyed, and we might no longer be enslaved to sin. For whoever has died is freed from sin. But if we have died with Christ, we believe that we will also live with him. We know that Christ, being raised from the dead, will never die again; death no longer has dominion over him. The death he died, he died to sin, once for all; but the life he lives, he lives to God. So you also must consider yourselves dead to sin and alive to God in Christ Jesus.

the world as those who have arisen from the water, we will be especially thankful for the radiance of the sun. Come and let us live as those who have just come up from the water. Stark naked, completely naked.

Art for Art's Sake (104)

I do not necessarily disapprove of art for art's sake. I want to tip my hat to grand efforts that sacrifice everything for the sake of beauty. But up until now, much of art for art's sake has stressed the sensuality of beauty, while giving little thought to the beauty of the soul, accentuating the beauty of the individual but not the beauty of the collectivity. A sensuality of beauty inclines toward hedonism and falls into the egoism of individual beauty. As a result, among those in the so-called art for art's sake group—who have sacrificed everything in the pursuit of beauty alone—are many who make the mistake of confusing art for art's sake with self-indulgent hedonism. Eternal beauty is conveyed only through the spirit of a whole life. I do not deny sensual beauty. But sensual beauty is not beauty in its entirety. Surely one important aspect of beauty is the eternal beauty dwelling in the soul's interior. Beauty evolves. As long as we view our own faces as beautiful and our neighbor's as blemished, only a partial beauty will appear on the earth. The campaign to beautify the neighbor's face is called morality. We must not forget that morality is also a factor in the shaping of art within the context of a whole life.

The Absolute Form in the Finite (107)

The space where absolute form appears in what is finite is the attractiveness of the religious life. The place where great, limitless power is revealed within a limited range is where life's mystery appears. From the perspective of the absolute, the limited world is a facet of the absolute. In God, everything is holy, and the importation of a sense of the holy into the life of senses is the key point of the incarnate life.[53] In the freedom of truth and with an open heart, the condition of a child of God is to lead the life of the senses without being tainted in the least bit by its depravity. In such a life sexual passion is united with holy purity, and the limited world shines like a flower opening at the tip of a branch. As the suffering at the tip of a branch is of no concern to the flower, those who know the mystery of incarnation are not bothered at all by the limited sphere of the senses. Even if betrayed by tears or death, the flower of the child of God blooms as profusely as the sunflower. If the reproductive function of plants can be loved as in a deep red blossom, why is human sexual desire alone felt to be so unsightly? Nevertheless, to those who begin with God, sexual desire is as lovely as the flower of the plant. No! It is through sexual desire we may come all the more into contact with the glorious light.

---

53. For the term "incarnate" here, rather than using the imported theological word 受肉 *juniku* ("took flesh"), Kagawa characteristically opts for the more familiar Buddhist term 化身 *keshin* ("made flesh").

The Japanese and Elegance (108)

In the Japanese love of beauty is a certain kind of beauty Westerners cannot comprehend. This is the beauty of elegance. The simplicity and depth of the beauty represented by elegance is indeed difficult for Westerners to grasp. I once translated Bashō's famous *haiku* into English and read it to some Americans:

Furu ike ya	An old pond
kawazu tobikomu	in leaps a frog
mizu no oto	sound of water.

They were at a complete loss as to what on earth this might mean. Westerners end up being completely flustered by *haiku* or *sumie* (ink wash painting). Western beauty is buoyant, Japanese beauty somber. Western beauty is sensual, Japanese beauty conceptual. Those who do perceive *kokoro*[54] in the interior depth of things cannot possibly comprehend Japanese beauty. As to the beauty of a tea ceremony room or a traditional Japanese garden, only one that deeply probes the *kokoro* has the sense of subtle grace needed to taste this beauty. Western beauty is something that can be grasped purely by sight. The more one savors Japanese beauty, the more its fragrance is enhanced. Western beauty is innocent and Japanese beauty closer to the time of maturity. I want to dwell forever in this elegance.

---

54. See note 1 above.

The Way of Tea (111)

There are few things that enhance the loveliness of life as much as the way of tea. The simple colors, the condition and appearance of the garden, the graceful architectural style, the refined curves of the tea utensils, the fragrant and complex flavors, the elegant perfumed aromas, the curvilinear beauty of carefully measured physical movements, the instant the iron kettle whistles out its alarm, the master's deliberate dipping of the ladle into the iron kettle and pouring just a little bit into a tea cup. The charming sound of tea being stirred. The southern sky cranes its neck to peek through the garden into the tea ceremony room. A winter wren comes near the pond for a drink of water. No word is spoken in the tea room and the *kokoro*[55] of host and guest melt together in the carefree pause for tea. It would be difficult to find anywhere in the world a plain beauty so simple and concentrated on life as the way of tea.

Our age has become frenzied. The dream of the tearoom has been disturbed. But the Japanese people will surely never be able to forget the spirit of the tearoom. There will certainly come a day when, at the very least, they will sit down and resolve to build teahouses.

---

55. See note 1 above.

Spirit has no National Boundaries (112)

There are no national boundaries to spirit. The Buddha is
neither Indian nor Japanese. He belongs to the world of the
spirit. It is exactly the same with Christ. Though born in Judea,
he does not belong to the Jews. He belongs to the earth. Rather,
he belongs to the whole world. Is there any national boundary
to Euclidean geometry? Are there territorial distinctions made
in electrical engineering? In knowledge and the ultimate
realm,[56] the presence or absence of a country's size or rulers
is not a problem. I have no problem with radical egalitarian
collectivism[57] with regard to knowledge and the *summum
bonum*.[58] In the realm of the spirit, we must not establish
national boundaries. While I am thankful for "Japanism,"[59] it
is futile to advocate conquest in the realm of the spirit. I am
happy for Japanese people to be self-consciously Japanese. There

56. For "the ultimate realm," Kagawa opts for the Buddhist-sounding phrase 最高の
世界 *saikō no sekai* rather than the Christian term 超越の世界 *chōetsu no sekai*, meaning
"transcendent realm."

57. He uses the Japanese word for "communism" here (共産主義 *kyōsanshugi*), but
I have rendered it as "radical egalitarian collectivism" for contextual reasons. From
the early 1920's Kagawa was at loggerheads with Japanese communists who chose a
confrontational and violent approach to social change. Because of his Christian faith
and his careful study of biological evolution, Kagawa opted for a more pacifist and
gradualist approach to social reform.

58. See note 9 above.

59. This admission of support for "Japanism" (original is 日本主義 *nihonshugi*) calls
for brief explanation. "Japanism" began as a nativist, cultural movement that opposed
the Meiji government's policy of Westernization. Its early ideological champions were
intellectuals such as Inoue Tetsujirō and Takayama Chogyū. After Japan's invasion of
China in the 1930's, it increasingly morphed into a virulent form of militaristic nation-
alism, which Kagawa opposed initially, yet to no avail. It is also important to recall
that the present book was published in 1926, just two years after the U.S. Congress
passed the infamous Immigration Act of 1924, or Johnson–Reed Act, the law aimed at
curtailing the immigration of Chinese and Japanese.

is no need to be obsessed with the culture of the West. But I am opposed to creating national boundaries to the truth or making distinctions in our love of humanity based on skin color. Spirit transcends territory and disregards skin color. The Spirit is a cosmopolitan citizen.

Not Everything in Nature is Beautiful (113)

Not everything in nature is beautiful. As it approaches human consciousness, nature changes shape. To those who are sad, even the glittering sun is an object of cursing, and to those filled with delight, the muddy open sewer running through the slum is a fountain of absolute pleasure. Nature does not speak heart to heart to those who do not cultivate the soul. To the utterly pure ancient peoples, mountains and rivers appeared as gods, and to medieval peoples imprisoned by dread and anxiety, nature was a nest of devils. It is only with modern people who understand and love nature that nature can be loved as nature for the first time. Breaking through to the bosom of God, we begin to make nature the domain of the self. The presence of love between the poet and the lilies of the field is the single thread of energy that links them together. The natural world cannot appear prior to the genesis of great love. We can say that those who love the spirit can for the first time love nature profoundly.

Politics and the Morality of the People (116)

It is said that politics is about the morality of the people.
It is utterly foolish to expect to see good government without
elevating the morality of the people. There are some who see
politics in terms of power. But while the politics of such people
may deteriorate, it will not advance. Expecting the nation to
produce good politicians in an immoral era is like expecting
grapes to appear from thistles. If a country were able to prosper
through power alone, no one would bother to sow seeds in the
field. The 2,700,000 pleasure seekers who frequent the red light
districts annually have sufficient power to plunge this country
into hell. Were politics alone able to reform the country, we
would not have needed Shinran[60] or Nichiren.[61] Before the
people are awakened, we have to stop the regular election process
that sends brothel owners and heads of crime syndicates to
the National Diet. And it is a huge error to say civilization has
arrived with the transfer of political power from rich comedians
to organized criminals. I think we first need to get moving on the
moral education of our citizens.

60. "(1173–1262) A Kamakura period monk, considered to be the founder of the *Jōdo Shin* school." *DDB.*
61. "(1222–1282) A Kamakura period monk who was a socially focused Buddhist and outspoken critic of current Buddhist practices and their teachers, who would end up becoming the founder of a school of Japanese Buddhism named after him, the *Nichiren shū* 日蓮宗, which is also known as the 法華宗 Lotus sect." *DDB.*

The Self-Consciousness of Faith and Love (117)

To believe means to be self-conscious of being loved. This means believing love is stronger than sickness, danger, and death. That is, though love may seem powerless, it means to believe it is more powerful than the sword. Because of this, we should not expect faith to have any advantage in itself. Faith as a psychological phenomenon is not necessarily an indication of redemptive salvation. The power for attaining redemption is solely a possession of the innate love that penetrates the cosmos. True religious faith is to be conscious that this power is working within me. We must not define religion too narrowly. We must think of religion as the movement of the whole of life that seeks to engender this innate love. Faith is no more than a bulb for the purpose of fully injecting the dynamic power of love into the carburetor of the spirit. Love is the reality of religion, faith its door.

Beginning from Zero (118)

If you just think about life for a moment, you realize that everything in the world, while beginning from nothing, has a truly delightful structure. When compared to the absence of life, even a small quantity of life is a world of great gain. Where two eyes are useless, the ears still remain.[62] If the ears are no good, the nose still remains. So long as a tiny something remains, there are riches compared to no life whatsoever. I am blessed with this mental attitude of abundance, and even if I suffered a kind of sorrow worse than hell's mountain of needles,[63] I still could not keep from blessing myself. I once thought it would be better to quickly depart this world of suffering, but then I thought more carefully and saw this idea was dramatic and very interesting when compared to nothing. In any event, it is better to have tears. Instead of the world of permanent nothingness, all things in the world are a benefit when I feel I am able to enjoy these tragic variations in outlook. There is nothing scary at all in the world. Tears, thorns, sickness, and death—it is all gain. Furthermore, life is crowned with the blessing of truth, light, beauty, and the *summun bonum*.[64] I press on without a care.

---

62. Recall these meditations were written during a period of blindness.
63. A Buddhist metaphorical depiction of a place where sinners are punished.
64. See note 9 above.

Love of Nature and Love of Humanity (119)

Some see the love of nature as born from a rebellion against human society. If you think like that, I suppose you will interpret things accordingly. We may perhaps call people selfish who throw off human society and think they alone will be favored by nature. But loving nature is actually a form of art. A mental outlook that wearies of unpleasant people and befriends the beautiful natural world is one way of participating in the art of the universe. But a cosmic art that does not include making human life more artistic is fragmentary. Even if one were to hide oneself in nature, if there is still some attachment to the self, such a love of nature does not necessarily free a person from what is human. Therefore, we cannot say lovers of nature are of a higher order than lovers of humanity. That is why we need a standard such as the perspective of cosmic art. From my own experience I honestly must confess, "The more I have loved nature, the more have I longed for people, and the more I have loved people, the more I have desired nature." Guy de Maupassant wrote that looking at the moon made him long for his lover, and this same feeling always wells up within me. While nature is good, so are people.

Serenity in the Inmost Heart (120)

When one is long immersed in the life of grace, there is a firm serenity deep in the heart that no one can disturb. Whether apprehended by five policemen, or placed under detention, in the middle of a street during a disturbance with a mob of 15,000, or about to be stabbed by a scoundrel's drawn sword,[65] the jewel of serenity hidden in my heart has not been shaken in the least. Even when an automobile I was riding in accidentally collided with a train and the train passed right over my head, I was able to maintain my composure. When chronic illness completely took away my eyesight, I did not see my stillness flutter. Like a well-polished mirror, the peaceful heart reflects every present situation just as it passes, but the surface of the mirror is not in the least bit disturbed. To me, infamy, abuse, scorn, or slander is nothing more than a polishing powder that makes the mirror of serenity shine brighter still.

I am amazed by this quietude that enables me to act like this. Earthquakes, fire alarms, blizzards, or avalanches cannot shake the absurdly calm and settled composure deep within my heart. I have witnessed too much meanness and too much sorrow. That is why this serenity cannot be disturbed by cruelty. There is but one thing and one thing alone that can shake my serenity. That is the inspiration of tears of love. Once it glimpses that pure love that seeks to redeem everything in sight, the fountain of my heart, in a shower of tears, produces ripples in my serenity like those

---

65. References to his arrest during the 1921 worker's strike at the Mitsubishi-Kawasaki Shipyard in Kobe and to being attacked in the slum. See Schildgen, *Toyohiko Kagawa*, 103–14, and especially 110 for a description of the arrest.

caused by a sudden and unexpected shower of rain on a lake's surface, which cannot be shaken by any offense or danger.

Possessing All Creation (122)

All creation is mine. I live by penetrating every created thing.
In the kitchen I am one with the spirit of the fire, one with the
spirit of the water, one with the spirit of the blazing range. All
things charm me, and I am fused with everything. I can dwell
in the soot in the chimney or find a peaceful place with the flea
under the tatami mat. Set free, I can fly upward to the Great Bear
Constellation, frolic from star to star, or hide myself under the
mirror on my lover's dresser. As long as I love the whole creation
I can travel about it with the utmost freedom. Mount Fuji and
the Japan Alps are wrinkles on my brow, the Atlantic and Pacific
Oceans are my robes. All creation is mine, the earth is one part
of my body,[66] and I hold the solar system in the palm of my hand

66. This meditation is reminiscent of Ming Neo-Confucian philosopher Wang
Yangming's (1472–1529) commentary on *The Great Learning*, a Confucian classic.
Kagawa thought highly of Wang Yangming and Nakae Tōju (1608–1648), the Japanese Neo-Confucian scholar who followed Wang's rejection of the dualism in the
ruling orthodoxy of Zhu Xi.

> The great man regards Heaven, Earth, and the myriad of things as one body.
> He regards the world as one family and the country as one person. . . . Forming
> one body with Heaven, Earth, and the myriad things is not only true of the
> great man. Even the mind of the small man is no different. . . . Therefore when
> he sees a child about to fall into a well, he cannot help a feeling of alarm and
> commiseration. This shows that his humanity forms one body with the child.
> It may be objected that the child belongs to the same species. Again, when he
> observes the pitiful cries and frightened appearance of birds and animals about
> to be slaughtered, he cannot help feeling an "inability to bear" their suffering.
> This shows that his humanity forms one body with birds and animals. It may
> be objected that birds and animals are sentient beings as he is. But when he sees
> plants broken and destroyed, he cannot help a feeling of pity. This shows that his
> humanity forms one body with the plants. It may be said that plants are living
> things as he is. Yet, even when he sees tiles and stones shattered and crushed, he
> cannot help a feeling of regret. This shows that his humanity forms one body
> with tiles and stones. This means that even the mind of the small man necessar-
> ily has the humanity that forms one body with all. Such a mind is rooted in his

and scatter millions of stars across the heavens. When God gave me Christ, all creation was thrown in as a gift.

Heaven-endowed nature, and is naturally intelligent, clear, and not beclouded. Wang Yangming "An Inquiry on the Great Learning," in *A Source Book in Chinese Philosophy*, translated and compiled by Wing-Tsit Chan (Princeton: Princeton University, 1963), 272.

Sin and Atheism (124)

To cover up their sin, those who have failed morally seek to deny God and God's reign. For this reason, as long as there is sin in the world, there will always be atheists. Among the many who proclaim atheism are those who become very serious and troubled should it turn out that God does exist. They seek to reject the extremely severe judgment of God. Leaving God out of the picture, they opt to behave according to their own whims. In short, they seek to make themselves into God. Of course, making themselves the norm, they adjust the standard for good and evil. According to their norm, everything inconvenient is evil, and everything agreeable, even adultery and stealing, is good. They are egomaniacs and megalomaniacs. The only standard for good and evil to be raised up must be the norm of eternal life, and this norm will not be lowered for any individual. God is eternal life and not a game manufactured by ideas. So let the atheists blow off steam. In the meantime, the gravity of life continually makes progress.

Morning (128)

Gandhi of India observes morning worship at 4:00 am, and as dawn approaches he gets sleepy and lies down again, showing that there is naturally some difference between spiritual practices in the tropics and spiritual experiences in temperate zones. During the Japanese summer, I think it is good for our spiritual life to follow the pattern of India. The environment for the optimal operation of human reason is about 65 degrees Fahrenheit, and in order to find that optimal temperature, the wisest observe religious worship early in the morning. Powerful revelations may also be given in the middle of the night, but there is a fear that continuing to meditate after a hard day's work might produce hallucinations as in a nervous breakdown. Following a restful night of sleep, praying with the morning star is the happiest part of being human. Jesus was a person who enjoyed the time before daybreak. I am happy that many who walk the path of Zen enjoy this same custom. I want to be a child of the dawn for all eternity.

A Single Grain of Wheat (129)

I am like a grain of wheat, which unless it falls into the earth and dies, remains just a single grain. But it was said that if it falls into the earth and dies, it bears much fruit.[67] I have discovered many things from the saints of Israel. Truly, the mystery of eternal life is the way of gain through loss. Saint Paul expresses this in the Letter to the Philippians.[68] I have no problem thinking of religion as learning that gain always follows loss, which is one provision of life's economics.[69] The Buddha preached Nirvana and powerfully taught us about loss. Jesus demonstrated it for us by means of the cross. The way of negation taught by the Buddha opened the complete affirmation of the path to enlightenment, and the cross of Jesus was the preamble to the resurrection. Truly, through having lost no more than just a little for God, I almost think there is no one so blessed as me, having become the possessor of unseen riches. Nothing teaches about making effective investments so

---

67. Kagawa applies John 12:24 to his own life and ministry. "Very truly, I tell you, unless a grain of wheat falls into the earth and dies, it remains just a single grain; but if it dies, it bears much fruit."

68. He is referring to the paradox of gain and loss in Philippians 3: 7–11.
   Yet whatever gains I had, these I have come to regard as loss because of Christ. More than that, I regard everything as loss because of the surpassing value of knowing Christ Jesus my Lord. For his sake I have suffered the loss of all things, and I regard them as rubbish, in order that I may gain Christ and be found in him, not having a righteousness of my own that comes from the law, but one that comes through faith in Christ, the righteousness from God based on faith. I want to know Christ and the power of his resurrection and the sharing of his sufferings by becoming like him in his death, if somehow I may attain the resurrection from the dead.

69. This odd-sounding term, "life's economics" 生命経済 *seimei keizai* is an example of the kind of intentional conflation Kagawa often makes between terms in religion, biology, economics, and other fields.

clearly as religion. Investing for God means an eternal return on your profit. Today's financiers who do not know this fact are themselves pitiable people.

I want to Love (130)

I want to love. This is becoming an even stronger instinct in me than wanting to be loved. From the time I was seven or eight until I was seventeen or eighteen, I was tormented by the desire to be loved. Now that I am nearing forty, the instinct to love others is stronger than the instinct of wanting others to love me. I do not think about wanting to be loved by my wife and children, but on the contrary, I desperately want to love them. While I do not know how long this feeling will persist, my guess is that it will last until I die. It seems I have been awakened to the parental instinct within me. The physiological reproductive function has given way to the psychological instinct for altruism, and deep within I forget about myself and seek to love others. Conscious of this mental activity, I feel there is no greater happiness than when I love my children. I feel completely desolate when my children are not present. I want to love. We may call this my creative desire.

Prophecy (133)

I am one of those who believe in prophecy regarding the fate of humanity. Kepler prophesied the existence of the orbits of planets in our solar system, and from the arrangement of atoms in the periodic table, Mendelev prophesied the discovery of new elements, and both these prophecies were later realized. Many earlier predictions about human behavior have also been realized. Even common people have thought that in the end the wicked perish while the good triumph, and this is surely the kind of prophecy that strikes the nail on the head in regard to decaying civilizations. From long ago, the prophets of Israel prophesied the downfall of their own country, and these all came to pass.[70] Examining the tendencies of history and projecting forward from these tendencies, we cannot say that predictions about the shape of the coming age are necessarily of an unscientific nature. To a pure conscience, the fate of a culture has a special and certain kind of precision as something that may be revealed. I believe in prophecy. Given the fates determined for the evil and the good, it is not so difficult through a well-polished conscience to discern a future inclination from a certain perspective. At the very least I can make the following prediction. Prostitution, alcohol, and crooked politics remove the root of a people, while, within a few years, the way of love, inventiveness, and peace is able to restore a people's vitality.

70. This was written in 1926, 22 years before the establishment of the modern state of Israel.

Life and Parasitism (138)

Unless one is exceptionally careful, the tendency to seek to live a parasitic life can quickly spring up in the main current of life. This happens in the human world when a clever person takes up the parasitic life and feels entitled to it as a right. Modern capitalism[71] is a striking example of this tendency, but it is not limited to capitalism. Parasitic life appears in every era and it takes a variety of forms. The only way to remedy this is to constantly take a faithful attitude toward the main current of life. In Israel, those who took a faithful attitude toward the main current of life came to be called prophets. Indeed, taking God as their norm, they criticized the contemporary age, and with no leniency for the wayward path of the people, they taught relentlessly. I believe we will never see the end of prophetic religion.

71. Kagawa has in mind here the Japanese 財閥 *zaibatsu*, meaning "financial cliques." They were a tiny group of powerful family monopolies that controlled industry and finance and exerted inordinate power on the domestic and foreign policies of the government.

A Mother's Breast (140)

There is nothing like a mother's breast. Why does it have such a beautiful protruding curve? It is not only our babies who want to cling to the breast. Becoming as a child once again, I also want to cling to my wife's breast. Are not all of the world's secrets here? My religion is nothing more and nothing less than this.[72] What a lovely picture! My child sucking away, clinging with mouth and nose squished into her mother's breast, which is bigger than her head, squeezing steadily with both hands. How many people have ever planned or produced such a beautiful scene? Even if the world is located at the bottom of the boiling pot of hell, here alone there dwells no demon or snake. As an eternal child, I want to cling to my wife's breast. My dear child, save a drop from your mother's nipple for me. I want to be a child of the breast forever.

72. See *Seeing All Things Whole*, 164–72, for a description of Kagawa's use of maternal metaphors to describe the human-divine relation.

The Curves of the Naked Body (142)

Among all of the clothing human beings have fashioned, why is there nothing so beautiful as the curves of the naked body? People have made various efforts, but do they not on the contrary diminish the gift of beauty given by God? I have never experienced a more impressive specimen of muscular beauty than when I stood in the British Museum in London before a Greek sculpture of a young boy cast from metal. It is more beautiful than anything else. Indeed, I keenly felt what Saint Paul had said about our flesh being a temple of God.[73] Later while viewing the sculptures at the Louvre in Paris, I was so utterly enchanted by the elegant lines of the beautiful naked body that it felt uncomfortable walking around in clothes. A joyful day for me is to let my completely naked son freely display his lovely curvaceousness. Liberated from clothing, my naked boy runs around the house full of joy. I think it would be great if the civilization of the beautiful naked body could once again replace that of artificial clothing. Lost in the Garden of Eden, will the

---

73. Reference to I Corinthians 6: 13–20, especially verse 19 (italicized below):
   "Food is meant for the stomach and the stomach for food," and God will destroy both one and the other. The body is meant not for fornication but for the Lord, and the Lord for the body. And God raised the Lord and will also raise us by his power. Do you not know that your bodies are members of Christ? Should I therefore take the members of Christ and make them members of a prostitute? Never! Do you not know that whoever is united to a prostitute becomes one body with her? For it is said, "The two shall be one flesh." But anyone united to the Lord becomes one spirit with him. Shun fornication! Every sin that a person commits is outside the body; but the fornicator sins against the body itself. *Or do you not know that your body is a temple of the Holy Spirit within you, which you have from God, and that you are not your own?* For you were bought with a price; therefore glorify God in your body.

beauty of the naked body ever return again? Until the sacred cleansing of our spirit is certain, it will surely not return to us.

A Pessimistic Ideology and the Suffocation of Life (144)

Those who sit at their desks and become prisoners of a pessimistic ideology should stand up at once. A gloomy ideology arises from the suffocation of life. No one who is active thinks, "It would be great to die." It is good for those obsessed with thinking of themselves to think a little of others. By doing so, Tolstoy was saved from committing suicide. It is good for sad people who are always confined to their studies to have a taste of nature's embrace. By doing so, John Stuart Mill escaped suicide. I never hear of a five or six year-old who planned to take their own life. A growing child has no time to think about things like suicide. If there remains even a little room for activity, life is enjoyable. Consider the child for whom throwing stones and spinning tops is great fun. It is good for you young people who embrace a pessimistic ideology to learn how to work with things and with people. The moment you do so your gloomy outlook will vanish.

I want to be a Child Again (145)

I want to see once again what it is like to be a child. Lighthearted, nimble, interested in everything, every muscle supple and fully functioning, even if sadness comes, forgetting it in an instant, talking with the stars, striking up a friendship with the violets, addressed by nymphs when visiting a pond, becoming chums with forest spirits when entering a forest, being shown special kindnesses by the dragon flies, butterflies, and grasshoppers—I would like to try being such a child.

As I age, my muscles harden and wrinkles appear on my skin, but why do I lose curiosity in everything and yawn continually at life? I want to be a child forever. I want to feel an eternal friendship with drops of rain, camellia blossoms, cicadas, and snowflakes. So long as my attraction to the child remains, I will be able to enjoy life on earth. I want to be eternally innocent and eternally curious. Truly, unless one is a child, one cannot enter the Kingdom of Heaven.[74]

74. A reference to Matthew 18: 1–5:
    At that time the disciples came to Jesus and asked, "Who is the greatest in the kingdom of heaven?" He called a child, whom he put among them, and said, "Truly I tell you, unless you change and become like children, you will never enter the kingdom of heaven. Whoever becomes humble like this child is the greatest in the kingdom of heaven. Whoever welcomes one such child in my name welcomes me."

Sickness and Boredom (146)

Intending to comfort me, someone told me, "Since you have so much work to accomplish, you must become bored with these long sicknesses." But I could not bring myself to confess I have felt any boredom in the least. I know I have a lot of work to do. But I do not live to work, rather I am given life to live. Thinking about tomorrow, I cannot be the kind of mindless idiot who spends the present moment being bored. My life is in this present moment. My current task is to be in this sickbed with God. I am not thinking about tomorrow or the day after tomorrow. Nor am I thinking about today's sunset. Without being bored, I am thinking in this moment only about being with God. I am ever giving thanks to God for the joy of living this moment together with God. There is no boredom in me.

Guarded by the "Vision of the Chariot of Fire" (147)

I always walk as far as I can. And when I feel the need to collapse, I gladly collapse. Unlike others, I do not think I want to die in my bed. Whether I die on the sea or in a train depends on the divine will. It is enough for me to do my very best. I am not in the least bit lonely. Even though I cannot see with my eyes, I am surrounded continuously by Elisha's "vision of the chariot of fire."[75] So long as I am with God, even a great army of a million men cannot put me to the sword. Along with the "vision of the chariot of fire," a wonderful power falls from heaven. Though I live in the electronic civilization of the twentieth century, I am a great fool who still believes Elisha's "vision of the chariot of fire." Even now I inhabit the myth. People are not likely to believe in myth. But I cannot keep from believing. I do not dwell at some long distance from the age of myth. On the contrary, I indwell the myth itself. Almost every day I see God's mysterious "vision of the chariot of fire."

75. See 2 Kings 2: 1–12.

Those Who Put God to the Test (148)

I have encountered a certain religious group that believes using medicine is an act of the devil, and they even prohibit medical treatment for victims of leprosy. When you compare the condition of hundreds of people who have received treatment with those who are not treated—purportedly because of believing in God—and they then collapse right before your eyes, I cannot suppress my pity. I know that they have strong faith. But, refusing treatment is no different than walking the Shikoku Pilgrimage.[76] This made me think. Jesus once said, "Do not put God to the test."[77] Even so, this group of people is putting God to the test. They are attempting to manipulate faith. This is a tragic contradiction. I for one believe modern science is a gift from God. To the last, I want to recognize the power of God through science. I also believe human strength is a gift of God.

---

76. The Shikoku Pilgrimage 四国遍路 *Shikoku Henro* is a pilgrimage of 88 temples associated with the Buddhist monk Kūkai (Kōbō Daishi) on the island of Shikoku.

77. The New Testament context is the wilderness temptation of Jesus, and the command, "Do not put God to the test" is directed at the devil (see Matt 4:1–11 and Luke 4:1–13).

The Personality of Objects (150)

If you think long enough about an object, you discover
that each object has its own personality. Even the brazier or the
charcoal box next to the desk in the study has a certain meaning
and each object speaks to its owner. Its shape, color, gloss, place
of production, materials, producers, users, the procedure for its
delivery, events that occurred in the object's surroundings—one
thing after another comes to mind. Things such as the oblong
brazier in the kitchen—there we find a single scratch made from
scraping up against it or a single stain on its surface—and all
of these things tell the deep history of a family. As years pass by
together with the brazier, it starts to take on its own personality.
This is where we get the notion that seeing someone's personal
belongings allows us to understand their character. To speak
three-dimensionally, if we enter the study of someone whose
possessions are all systematically ordered, we get a good sense of
the what is truly important to that person.

Just as a person exercises a great influence on certain objects,
objects may exercise a great influence on persons. Everyone
knows a garish color irritates the human heart while an elegant
color has a calming influence. When the *shimenawa*[78] is put up,
it feels like the New Year, and when the *koinobori*[79] is raised, we
naturally feel in high spirits. Objects have great power to inspire.
When seated before inanimate objects I never speak of as mere
objects, the Infinite One takes various forms and draws near to

78. A Shinto rope used to cordon off consecrated areas or as a talisman against evil.
79. Colorful carp banners used as decorations for Children's Day (formerly Boy's Day) on May 5.

my heart. So long as I have inanimate objects as friends, I will never be sad.

The Limitations of Technical Civilization (152)

Whenever I return to the city from the countryside, it always occurs to me that modern civilization unfortunately has come to the end of its tether. While things have become more convenient and well designed, one cannot deny that simplicity and human warmth are gradually disappearing. Having said that, by no means am I among those who reject technical civilization. However, I am one who prefers the satisfaction of holding one handmade rice bowl to five produced by a machine. Regardless of how well it is made, after a certain point I loose interest in the machine made cup. I never tire of looking at a cup made by human hands, even if there is some imperfection in its shape. If we were to enter a medieval city, though we would find none of the conveniences of modern cities, we would be struck by the human affection present in a single stone or a single brick. Here I feel a profound intimacy. A city with a population of about thirty thousand is just the right size. If it gets bigger than that, I am afraid things will heat up. It seems it would be wise for people to moderate their desires in order to live more comfortably.

Standing under a Waterfall (153)

Once when I had gone to receive medical treatment from a certain doctor, he said the following words to me. "Beyond a certain point, there is no other way except for nature to perform the healing. Since most doctors these days think only about a disease's pathology and not its treatment, religious forms of treatment that have come down to us through thousands of years are far and away more likely to be effective than an unskilled physician. One of those practices, for example, is that of standing under a waterfall and being pounded by the intense force of the water." I immediately thought about the groups of pilgrims who stand under waterfalls as a religious practice. Indeed, compared with modern medicine, the ascetic experience of completely losing oneself while being pounded by a mountainside waterfall is far more mystical and extraordinary. At times when human ability has reached its limit, there may be nothing left to do but to stand under a waterfall. Medicines do not cure human sicknesses, but the body's cells, which are stimulated by medicines, do the healing. If we think deeply about it, the human part in healing is far exceeded by God's part, thus we should expect everything to be resolvable if we turn it over to nature and God. Humans play only a subordinate role.

The Wolf of Suffering (156)

The wolf of suffering incessantly chases after me as one plagued by the demon of ill health. I am very well acquainted with this wolf's frightening fangs. Because of that I run at full speed just to stay one step ahead of him. I cannot say how long I will be able to outrun him, but when I look back on how I have managed to escape thus far, I also realize I must keep running from here on out. Come and get me, wolf of suffering! I will keep one step ahead of you! Because of these extreme troubles, I have never felt fatigue. Thus I am compelled to give thanks to God for this constant anxiety. I have only taken a little money for myself. Yet I feel ashamed when I see how many people have absolutely nothing while I have something, and then I give it all away. And then once again, the wolf of suffering chases after me. If I think about it, those who suffer with nothing have it easier than those who have something and yet are anxious. I am determined to continue like this as long as God gives me strength to stay just one step ahead of the wolf. When hard pressed, I am closest to God, and being close to God is for me the greatest happiness, so though the wolf is terrifying, I will continue to escape him until I collapse. Anything beyond that point depends on God's will. While being chased by the wolf, and though I am blind, I will believe in God's guidance and run with all my might in the darkness. So long as I am able to escape, my life is a life of victory.

A Gambler for God (157)

I know how to live comfortably. So long as things are going smoothly, life is not so difficult. But in a time like this when so many people are suffering, by no means am I able to live in comfort. Like a gambler, I stake everything on God. All of my earnings are pressed into the Kingdom of God Movement.[80] If a grain of wheat is not sown, it will not return one hundred fold. Like the gamblers whom I closely observed in the slum, I make my bets, only for a good purpose. Unless I abandon all, I will not know whether I will become naked or win the victory. So I gambled. Possessions, status, and honor, I bet it all on God. Whether the coin toss will come up evens or odds depends on God's will. The reason I am poor is because I am a gambler. The prophet Jeremiah called himself a drunkard for God,[81] but I call myself God's gambler. I have staked everything on God.

80. The nationwide evangelistic movement that Kagawa launched in 1926 and led until the early 1930's.
81. Jeremiah 23: 9:
Concerning the prophets: My heart is crushed within me, all my bones shake; I have become like a drunkard, like one overcome by wine, because of the LORD and because of his holy words."

Where to Throw Away One's Life (161)

In Japan, there has recently been a striking increase in the number of suicide victims. I fear it is probable there will be 15,000 suicides this year. The newspaper reports that every three hours eight people commit suicide in Tokyo. When I researched the causes of suicides in Japan, up to half of the many victims had some physical or psychological disease. Another ten percent kill themselves out of despair or weariness with life. This being the case, it is often said that many women are dying because they are faint of heart, but why then are young men nearly twice as likely to kill themselves when compared with women? I want to shout out before our entire nation. We must live strongly. To live strongly is called religion. Hence, the citizens of Japan must live religiously. We must embark on an even mightier adventure with an even stronger altruism, and rather than wasting away in the lifeless city districts, we must live powerfully under the care of Mother Nature. Our lives that are destined to die should be tossed away there, in the arms of Mother Nature. The plains of Hokkaido and the waves of the Pacific Ocean are not so confined that they can't receive our bodies when they are ready for burial. If the youth of Japan are throwing away their lives on the rat poison and the noose, why not by all means devote your lives to the vast fields and seas to be cultivated or to the poor and the slums?

Lonely Days (163)

I have spent very many days being lonely. Since I lost both my father and mother as a young boy, as a child I very rarely felt the love of flesh and blood.[82] I spent a year alone in a tuberculosis hospital and fishing village and lived for six months by myself on a plateau in Utah in North America. Because of this, I have had considerable time to think about loneliness. When I am feeling desolate, if I give myself to study or pray really hard, I completely forget about being lonely. I feel the most intense desolation when my mental state will not settle down, I am troubled by all sorts of wild delusions, and I cannot pray, study, or sit in silent meditation. One time when my mental state simply would not settle down was when I was frightened, thinking I heard a ghost calling me from the corner of the room. Hence, I think one must first endeavor to obtain peace of mind in order to overcome loneliness.

---

82. See *Seeing All Things Whole*, 17–47.

The Idea of Being Reborn in Another World (164)

A certain religious sect excommunicated a person who claimed that the idea of being reborn after death[83] is not the core of religion. Surely, for those who seek to live unreservedly, the immortality of the soul does not constitute the core of religion. Those who ponder the immortality of the soul place self first and God second. From my perspective, the idea of being reborn after death is a very self-indulgent ideology. By no means is it the *summun bonum*[84] of religious ideas. Whether or not there is life after death, we can say that serious religious faith is obedience to God, and therein is absolute devotion. At the same time, I do not say that the religious idea of being reborn after death, which places immortality of the soul at the center, is somehow irreligious. While it is probably not a religion fostering the creation of values, it is surely a religion fostering the preservation of values.[85] While being grateful for the joy of preservation, the ingenious solution of life is more certain.[86]

83. 往生思想 Ōjō Shisō "Being reborn (in another world). In most cases, this term is seen used in reference to the attainment of rebirth in a positive sense, such as rebirth into a pure buddha-realm, or into a heaven, etc. In colloquial writing however, it can refer simply to the notion of death. It is most commonly seen used in Pure Land texts, indicating rebirth into Sukhāvatī or some other pure realm based on virtuous behavior and religious practices in the present lifetime." *DDB*.

84. See note 9 above.

85. While these phrases are slightly awkward in English, Kagawa regularly contrasts dynamic "religious movements for the creation of values" 価値創造の宗教運動 *kachi sōzō no shūkyō undō* with static "religious movements for the preservation of values" 価値保存の宗教運動 *kachi hozon no shūkyō undō*.

86. He does not reject the conservative function of religion but sees religions that do not engender a vibrant spiritual creativity and progress in the face of developments in culture and challenges in contemporary life as woefully inadequate. The "ingenious solution of life" 生命の工夫 *seimei no kufū* is another key Kagawa phrase that is influenced by French philosopher Henri Bergson's notion of the *élan vital*; which Kagawa

When We are Out of Tune (166)

When one is out of tune, many sins press in on us. Sin comes in at times we become too prideful, or over confident, or we pretend to know something when we do not, or we want it to appear we have won when we have lost. The origin of adultery is conceit, and the source of theft is vanity. Murder comes from thinking you alone are good, and lying and covetousness arise from the desire to live someone else's life and not your own. It is all rooted in wanting to live a double life, but such a state of affairs is not possible for those who accept themselves just as they are and want to show themselves to others just as they are. There is no falsehood in those filled with the innocence of the innocent, and in those without conceit there is no need to commit adultery. Those who think humbly of themselves do not have the courage to kill a person nor do they fantasize about another woman falling in love with them. The desire to steal and covetousness does not occur to those who are not show offs. Sin occurs where too much weight is given to showing off the external appearance. That is, every sin has its source in vanity. Without exception, all homicidal devils are prisoners of vanity, and all adulterers worship at the altar of conceit. There is no sin in those who hold loosely to externals. I was born a child of vanity and lived in the midst of vanity. But now I am delighted to be free of it all.

---

critically takes on. See *Seeing All Things Whole*, 63–4, 148–51.

Invertebrates and Property Rights (169)

There is nothing as laughable in the world as property rights. For a child, a piece of glass is better than a diamond, and to a miser, a tiny gold coin more precious than inventive insight. That is, property rights may be seen as something that reflects human purpose at a given point of time. As a result, for people whose purpose is creating, property rights do not become an issue, and for those who invent, a tiny piece of glass or gold is not necessarily something of value. Property rights are something like the shell of a shellfish. Those who make a profit from them try to keep them hidden for themselves, but for those who are seeking higher ground by standing on tiptoe, they are nothing but an obstacle. As a shell that exists for the sake of a mollusk, we may say that people who stick to property rights are spineless invertebrates. In an age of invention and discovery, it is natural for an ideology of ownership advocated by mollusks to be shaken severely. This makes me feel sad for mollusks.

Life as the Absolute God (176)

God should not be thought of as an abstraction. God is living itself. And living means to be given life. That which is given life is the human and that which gives live is life itself. Even those who do not posit God objectively or those who view the universe as an illusion cannot deny the singular fact that they are living. We are living. I do not posit God objectively. I think of God as life itself. Life penetrates me and eternally moves ahead. This eternal life is God. Even those who objectively deny God cannot deny the existence of life. In reality life is absolute. Life carries out its purpose in "me." That is, life is personal. Is there anything strange about calling this purposeful, absolute life God? In me, God is neither objective nor subjective but absolute as life.

Affirmation and Mahayana Thought (179)

Recently in the West, people have appeared who have a deep respect for Indian religion. Indian religion finds its essence in the doctrine of negation. In the wake of ww i, it is not without reason that the West has grown weary of an excessively positive view of life, which is as ephemeral as a dragonfly, and is singing the praises of the extremely negative Indian ideology. Of course, a negativism that promises security is far and away happier than a positivism that leads to destruction. Having said that, even while denying reality, a contradictory negative view of life that eventually eats away at reality must someday itself be amended by the affirmation of Mahayana[87] thought. Before being guided by the Mahayana way, and rather than negating the struggle for supremacy or a sensual ideology, a leap forward to an affirmation of the introspection and self-awareness that characterizes a life of conscience will require more than a simple intellectual game. The world of life will always be the Mahayana ideology. But an intellectual Mahayana does not necessary welcome this fact. Life transcends negation and affirmation and commands us to surge ahead toward the ideal world.

87. Mahayana is the form of Buddhism that spread through China, Korea, and Japan.

Education in Love (181)

Just as a mother bird teaches her chicks how to eat, human beings must teach their children how to love other people. Even with the chick's instinctive desire to eat, they must still be taught to distinguish foods. So it is with regard to kindness, which must be adequately taught. People have the propensity to be selfish and the propensity to love others. We have variable instincts as lovers, parents, friends, or citizens, and without guidance we will not see the full flowering of these loves. In Japan, there is absolutely zero education in love. While going so far as to teach the love of Japan, elementary schools do not teach the love of the world, the love of sinners, and certainly not the love of barbarians. Here the social morality in Japan is inadequate.[88] It is difficult to discover the image of the perfect God where there is no knowledge of love. I must begin by teaching love to kindergarten children while they are at play.[89]

---

88. This is a clear criticism of the failure of the moral education 修身 *shūshin* curriculum used in all public schools of the day, which emphasized family virtues and patriotic sentiments but shunned universal values.

89. With young children in his own family, Kagawa now turns to the task of religious education, writing a succession of books on the subject in the late 1920's and early 1930's, and founding the Matsuzawa Kindergarten in 1931. In 1999, Kagawa was posthumously selected by UNICEF as one of 52 world leaders who exercised "Leadership in the best interests of the child." (http://www.unicef.org/sowc00/int1.htm)

Professional Religionists and the Fall of Religion (182)

I feel no heartfelt respect whatsoever for professional religionists. Where disputes about doctrine and dogma are repeated endlessly, but there is no discussion of the best ways to practice charity, how can we ever expect to discover the kind of religion of life that warms the human blood? The reason today's so-called religious universities are imparting useless learning is because they are fixated on the higher criticism of doctrine and dogma. Doctrine and dogma are clothing, they are not life itself. Accordingly, whenever true religion rejects professional religionists and teaches the democratization of faith, it begins to discover the religion of life. Christ was a carpenter, not a graduate of the Jerusalem theological school. Francis (of Assisi) was a wounded horseman, not a teacher of papal law. Whenever we entrust faith to religious professionals alone, the fall of religion begins.

Women and Eternity (183)

We need to note carefully that women all around the world have a strong religious tendency. When we look at churches in the West, there are few congregations where women do not make up two thirds of the membership. The question of why women have this religious disposition is a point that should be carefully contemplated. It is not because, when compared with men, they are said to have a weaker nature or are more emotional. Is it not because they are in a position to think more deeply about the mysteries of life? The three great activities of pregnancy, childbirth, and nursing cause them to think deeply about life, and with their responsibility as mothers, they desire to guide their children in the pure ways of God. I simply cannot bring myself to conclude that religion is emotional because women believe it. On the contrary, precisely because they believe I think of them as superior and as bearers of eternity. Men exist for a single generation, while women think about the next generation.

The Prophets are Killed in Jerusalem (187)

Jesus said that the prophets are killed in Jerusalem, and I for one believe what he said. Government does not arise out of the real life of the people, thus as long as governing is left in the hands of so-called politicians, it will assume the character of sport. This is why those who live in centers of government cannot avoid being infected by the system of exploitation of dancing illusionists running the self-styled "political sport." Even if one is not killed on a cross, living in Jerusalem will lead to the death of the spirit. Because they become infected by political sport, labor leaders who become political traders always end up falling. The more they are detached from real life, immersed in political sport, and suffer the disease of authoritarianism, even those who start out with sincere motives end up living as parasites. This same psychology drives anarchistic activists who set out to exterminate all devils but then themselves become the world's most frightening devils. It is safest to think of prophets as useless in their hometowns or in Jerusalem. It is best for sport to remain forever a sport.

The Dearth of Introspection in the City (188)

Those who are too busy even lose the chance to hear the
voice of conscience. There are so many juvenile delinquents
in our cities because we do not provide children occasions for
introspection. For this same reason, there are so many murderers
in the United States, the most technically advanced civilization.
The same principle appears among modern people who are
isolated from nature and have no opportunity for reflection.
Many people are likely to laugh at the idea of introspection.
Once when I suggested it would be better for American women
to be quieter, a certain American woman laughed in my face.
Through being silent, an excited state of mind is calmed,
mistakes in judgment avoided, and in thinking about past
and future, the proper course of action more clearly revealed.
Introspection is the meditation hall[90] for attending to God's
voice. When it is lost, religion vanishes.

90. 道場 *dōjō*, "Site of enlightenment. The place where enlightenment is achieved.
This refers initially to the ground under the bodhi tree, where the Buddha was seated at
the time of achieving his full enlightenment (Skt. *bodhi-manda*)." DDB.

In Praise of the Savage (189)

Following various tiresome artistic movements, the appearance of the movement in praise of the savage such as that of Gauguin is of great interest. Having suffered a failure of nerve, it was necessary for the arts to get naked again. Liberated from the imprisonment to line and color, there was a need for a return to the severe, primitive ambience. Yet because art that is guided mainly by mood follows the stimulus of the curve, it is constantly changing and excessively troubled and enchained by convention and style, so it turns out to be short lived and worthless when an artistic movement arises that places life at the center. Before the true art of the spirit, a mostly playful, taste-centered art is exposed as almost completely worthless. There is a great distance between so-called skillful craftsmanship and authentic art. Authentic art is eternal and spiritual, while so-called skillful craftsmanship is far removed from life like a day-old newspaper. The art that I long for is the art of life itself, which straightaway leads us into the realm of religion.

That which is Stronger than Love (190)

There is something stronger than love, and that something is faith. It is not necessarily unusual for someone to die for love. But most of those deaths do not indicate the victory of love. On the contrary, there is something far stronger in those who die for faith, inasmuch as it signals victory, than in those who die out of love. If love is blind, faith is super-blind. I have not heard of the population of Europe decreasing by one third for the sake of love. But because of faith, we hear that Europe's population did decrease by a third during the Thirty-Years War. I know that love is an immense power in human life. But I laugh at those who theorize that love is all there is. Religion signifies life itself, while love tells us about one dimension of life. There truly is something greater than love. That is the will to live, and the will to live is the determination to become God. This is faith.

Life, Growth, and Prayer (191)

I pray. Yet I am not immune to the philosophical question of whether prayer is a good or bad thing. But I do not pray because it is philosophical to pray. I pray because I am alive. It seems I am created for growth. But growing things have certain needs. I present my needs before the Lord of life. That is my prayer. I pray to God about everything. But I do not pray merely about my own happiness. I pray for the completion of God's initiatives. The prophet Jeremiah said that if God did not hear his prayer, he would appeal to God's reputation. This is how I think, too. I make demands. I make strong demands. While in prayer, I believe God absolutely hears my prayer. That is because I do not pray for myself. And I do not feel the least bit of loss if my prayer is not answered. That is because I do not pray for myself. If my prayer is not answered, I see it as God's plan being postponed. I pray.

The Lotus Sutra and Democracy (192)

When I read the Lotus Sutra, I feel I am getting to know a powerful family. Through the influence of the Lotus Sutra, the patriot Nichiren prayed for the safety of his country, which appears to be a stark difference from today's Nichiren ideologues who are flattered by those in authority. At least, this much is true: Nichiren was a friend of the weak. Given this stark difference, Nichiren himself is weeping in the grave for today's Nichiren ideologues that only peddle militarism without touching on the true meaning of faith. The spirit of the Lotus Sutra is a spirit of deep reverence that does not look down on all sentient beings.[91] This is precisely where we find a democratic impulse in the Lotus Sutra. Does the Lotus Sutra really preach the idolization of power or siding with the strong? Does the Lotus Sutra command the release of dozens of criminal detainees and murderers on the evening of the memorial service for Nichiren?[92] On behalf of the reputation of the Lotus Sutra, I will cry out for true democracy.[93]

91. 常不軽 *jōfugyō*. "Never despise. Senses: 1.) To never look down upon; never take lightly (Skt. *sadā-paribhūta, sada-paribhūta*); and 2.) *Sadāparibhūta*. The name of a bodhisattva in the Lotus Sutra; this was also a name of Śākyamuni in one of his previous lifetimes as a bodhisattva, when he saw the equality in all beings in their possession of the buddha-nature." *DDB*.

92. Memorial service for Nichiren held on October 13. This seems to be a reference to a recent historical event. Kagawa was often critical of religious leaders, and here he bemoans the release of certain persons of questionable character with the full support of certain "Nichiren ideologues."

93. Hopes for democracy were high in Japan during the 1920's, but economic and political realities gradually favored the militarists during the early 1930's.

Life on Mars (193)

If there happens to be functioning, intelligent life on Mars, I believe it will be virtually the same, in terms of its physiological organization, as the human life that inhabits the earth. Even if the laws governing the universe are innumerable, the law of life cannot be so variable. Even among species that are somewhat different, it does indeed seem a wonder of wonders that they resemble each other to some extent. Though a great distance separates Earth and Mars, I believe it is likely that the law of life maintained on both planets follows the same principle. Also, there is surely not much difference in the tendencies of evolution in both places. The reason I say this is not based purely on imagination, but it is because there is always a single law present even when examining tendencies among organisms with many differences.[94] Law transcends space. Thus there is likely to be little difference between life on Earth and on Mars.

94. Kagawa had taken advanced courses in biology at Princeton University from 1914–1916 just after the 1913 publication of Lawrence Henderson's *The Fitness of the Environment*. In his examination of the delicate relationship between water and life in the environment, Henderson was one of the first to argue for "fine-tuning" in the universe, an idea that resonated with Kagawa's Christian convictions, as well as his Neo-Confucian and Buddhist cultural heritage. Kagawa includes a translation of a long section from Henderson's book in *Cosmic Purpose*, 104–109.

Saint Paul's Possession of No Possessions (195)

I discovered a curious expression in Saint Paul's writings. In his Epistle to the Romans he teaches that we possess all things, and also in the two Epistles to the Corinthians, he says, "So let no one boast.... For all things are yours... whether the world or life or death or the present or the future—all belong to you,"[95] and "having nothing, and yet possessing everything."[96] I always find myself rethinking things when I consider the astonishing breadth of Saint Paul's mind in his claim to possess all things. Apart from teaching God, is there any other way to understand true possessions? The notion that all of the world's possessions are returned to one who possesses nothing is an interesting view of possessions. In the end, short of a return to Paul's teaching, nothing whatsoever will come of private property or communist-based systems.

95. 1 Corinthians 3:21–22.
96. 2 Corinthians 6:10.

Heirs of the Kingdom of God (196)

Our son is a poet. He sings incomprehensibly and then announces gleefully that it is his own composition. He makes my arm into a pillow for his head and says poetic things such as, "If I tap my ear on Papa's arm, I hear a song come out from inside." He is now three years and eight months old. Without having to call on the main character in Maeterlinck's play "The Blue Bird," my little boy leads me into the spirit world. Our son leads me into the "world of forgetfulness" and accompanies me to the "world of mirrors." It is no surprise that the saints say you will never enter heaven unless you truly become as a little child. Claiming that the spiritless incoherent tales of the aged make up moral education, ethics, discretion, or sincerity will never bring the ideal of human perfection any closer. Filled with a youthful energy that springs forward and becomes a child, will we not see the first sure budding of human perfection?

Japan's Gentle Religious Images (197)

I have made a discovery. The Japanese are not a nation who put up with cruelty. In all of the religious images in Japan, one does not see horrific figures such as India's *Kali*, nor does one hear brutal tales such as those of China. The Japanese like images such as *Nyorai*[97] and *Kannon*.[98] Human beings cannot worship that which is not in keeping with their true character. Perhaps Japanese like stories of avenging foes because we have not awakened yet from the dream of the age of feudalism. Yet I cannot deny that in the depths of the Japanese soul are faces resembling the images of *Nyorai* and *Kannon*. The Japanese are a gentle people in the bottom of their souls. Some have taken them to be a war-like nation. It is a mistake to worship idols. Yet we must not confuse peoples who worship *Nyorai* and *Kannon* with those who worship *Kali* and *Tyr* (ancient Germanic idol). *Nyorai* and *Kannon* are the soul of Japan. Religious images are no more than a reflection of the soul.

97. 如来, *Tathāgata* (Sanskrit). A term applied to those who, like the Buddha, have achieved enlightenment.

98. 観音, *Avalokiteśvara* (Sanskrit). Bodhisattva or Goddess of mercy and compassion.

The God Who Appears in Dreams (198)

Once again, I awoke this morning deep in prayer. After drifting off to a quiet sleep during my evening prayers, the unfamiliar path of my dream conveyed me through the naked darkness to God and to the Holy, and I passed most peacefully through a field of deep violet. When I woke up from my dream in the morning, I parted with the loving God and the Holy, greeting the shadows of dawn with misty eyes.[99] After spending such a peaceful night with God, I could not help feeling somewhat afraid when that peace was broken by the return to reality. Having been accompanied by God through darkness, dream, and meditation, I thought, if this kind of peace could be sustained, I might even pray to God to remain blind. Quietly, so quietly, my sun rises. And in this exceedingly hurried and troublesome world, I have to be careful so the serenity gained in the darkness will not be broken. But the real world is also a great revelation to me. However, there is an extreme absence of relationality in the world seen with two eyes. I cannot rely solely on my eyes. I will choose the dark night in order to sense God in all of life. There I am enabled to meet with God in fullness.

99. Recall that Kagawa dictated these meditations during a period of temporary blindness.

No Need to Hide One's Strengths (199)

I do not recognize a need for being pessimistic at all. Do I not have sufficient strength to overcome temptations? What about that time in the Parisian public house when a naked young French woman embraced me by the neck; did I not think of her as a dangling doll and in the very next moment figure out how best to pray for her? Many say the flesh overpowers the spirit, but I have had the opposite experience.

If I were allowed an honest confession, contrary to expectations it would be that I see no need to hide one's strengths. Why do the writers of the world only accentuate weakness in their literature? If authentic confession had literary value, I would want to boast of my strengths. The Holy within me will not listen to excessive pleas to indulge in momentary pleasures. So I will confess. As one captivated by God, I am no longer able to hand over my spirit to obscene thoughts. I will boast, boast in the strength of the "God" within me.

I Have Eyes over my Whole Body (200)

"O my soul, do you hear God's expression of concern for suffering in the universe?"

"Yes I hear, I hear. Ever since closing my eyes, I have sensed the pulse of cosmic life from within, and indeed I hear the deep groaning of the divine breath. The answer rises in my heart that God is the possessor of a powerful will, exerting every possible effort to make all things grow, restore those who have veered into a wrong path, and rescue those who have strayed into a nearby path. Like the tremor of an earthquake, the powerful groaning of God reverberates in my heart. While I did not sense it so much when I could see with my two open eyes, the longer I have sat in the darkness the more have I sensed this strong trembling through my whole body. That is, having lost the sight in both of my eyes, I cannot help but feel as if my eyes have expanded across my entire body. I feel it, like electricity I feel the powerful strength of divine creation and regeneration flooding my body. Indeed, God is life itself. God is the love within which I grow.

72964415R00088

Made in the USA
Lexington, KY
05 December 2017